South Yorkshire Mining Villages

The history of the region's coal mining villages is not only about places but also about people, many of them migrants. Shown here are William and Elizabeth Vernon. William was born in the hamlet of Micklebring just north of Maltby in 1829, and his wife was born in Wadworth a few miles to the north-east in 1837. The photograph shows them in later life. After their marriage they migrated just 13 miles westwards where William was employed by Newton Chambers & Co Ltd. William Vernon has two claims to fame. It was he who blew the buzzer at Tankersley Colliery on 21 January 1870, in his capacity as 'engine tenter', to warn troops and police in Barnsley that riots were taking place during the Thorncliffe lock-out of 1869–70. He then hid under the floorboards in the engine house. (see Chapter 2). His second claim to fame is that in later life he became a grocer and founded the first co-operative store in the Chapeltown area on Warren Lane (see also Chapter 2) in the Vernons' own cottage.

South Yorkshire Mining Villages

A History of the Region's Former Coal Mining Communities

Melvyn Jones

PEN & SWORD HISTORY

First published in Great Britain in 2017 by
Pen & Sword History
an imprint of
Pen & Sword Books Ltd
47 Church Street
Barnsley
South Yorkshire
S70 2AS

ISBN 978 1 47388 077 1

Typeset in Ehrhardt by
Mac Style Ltd, Bridlington, East Yorkshire
Printed and bound in the UK by CPI Group (UK) Ltd,
Croydon, CR0 4YY

Pen & Sword Books Ltd incorporates the imprints of Pen & Sword Archaeology, Atlas,
Aviation, Battleground, Discovery, Family History, History, Maritime, Military, Naval,
Politics, Railways, Select, Transport, True Crime, Fiction, Frontline Books, Leo Cooper,
Praetorian Press, Seaforth Publishing and Wharncliffe.

For a complete list of Pen & Sword titles please contact
PEN & SWORD BOOKS LIMITED
47 Church Street, Barnsley, South Yorkshire, S70 2AS, England
E-mail: enquiries@pen-and-sword.co.uk
Website: www.pen-and-sword.co.uk

Contents

Foreword

At the outset I think I ought to declare my interest in the coal mining communities of South Yorkshire. My great-grandfather on my mother's side, Charles Seargent, was a miner who migrated to the Barnsley district at the end of the 1870s from the Tipton area of Staffordshire. My grandfather was born in Barnsley, when they were living on Gilchrist Terrace off Cemetery Road, but two of his brothers were born in Woolley. My great-grandfather worked at Barnsley Main in the early 1880s. They then migrated again in 1885, this time to Australia, where my great-grandfather worked in the mining industry in the town of Lithgow, 93 miles west of Sydney in New South Wales. After about a decade they'd had enough (or made enough money!) and came back to England – to Barnsley. But not in the mines; my great-grandfather became a pub landlord, at the *Shepherd's Rest* in Heelis Street. He also owned property in Kingstone on the outskirts of Barnsley.

His son, Arthur, my grandfather, however, who had been born in South Yorkshire but brought up in Australia, became a coal miner at Barnsley Main and remained there for the rest of his working life. He married Emily Dryden, the granddaughter of George Dryden, the son of a linen handloom weaver, John Dryden, who had moved with his family progressively southwards from Darlington, to Northallerton, Knaresborough and Leeds. By the time of the 1851 census they were living and working in Barnsley. But the handloom linen industry was in rapid decline and linen manufacturing was becoming a factory industry that overwhelmingly employed girls and women to look after the looms. So George, who like his father had started his working life as a handloom weaver working in the family cellar on his loom, became a miner and went to live in Worsbrough Bridge. He was killed while sinking an ironstone mine at Rockley in 1863.

Two decades later, in the summer of 1884 in north Wales, a large colliery beside the River Dee, Mostyn Quay Colliery, was flooded and it never became operational again. This led to much out-migration of miners and their families to work in other north Wales collieries, to England and beyond (to the USA and Argentina). Most migrants to England went to the Lancashire coalfield. But in the same year that Mostyn Quay Colliery was flooded, a Mostyn man, Evan Parry, was appointed manager at Old Carlton Colliery in South Yorkshire. Some of his relatives joined him, they were joined by friends and neighbours and soon there was a Welsh colony in Carlton and neighbouring Smithies (see Chapter 4). My grandfather, Robert Samuel Jones and his wife and two boys, came to Smithies in 1903 from Mostyn via Parr in Lancashire. They lived at first on the Old Road in Smithies, along with other migrants from north Wales and Robert Samuel worked at

Barnsley Main. Eventually they had a family of eight including six boys: David, Emrys, Herbert, Edwin, Howell and Robert (my father) all but one of whom were miners for all or part of their working lives. David, the eldest son, survived the explosion at North Gawber in 1936. My dad also worked at North Gawber at that time but was not in the pit at the time of the explosion. Emrys died in 1941 from injuries following a pit accident.

I grew up in a mining family. My dad worked in local collieries (Old Carlton, North Gawber, Monk Bretton and New Carlton) for more than fifty years. We lived on a council estate in Smithies, but it was basically a mining village with most of the heads of household and often their sons working in local pits. Tommy Roberts' pit paddy (a lorry with a tarpaulin roof and forms on both sides), used to stop on the main road opposite our house to pick up and drop off miners working at the Old Carlton and New Carlton pits. The first excursion I went on after the war was to Baslow in a Tommy Roberts' pit paddy – in the pouring rain! And every month a ton of coal was tipped at the gate which had to be carried along the path in buckets and piled up in the 'coil 'oil'. During the Second World War 'Bevin Huts' were built in Smithies, between New Lane and New Hill Road to accommodate Bevin Boys, i.e. young men conscripted for the armed forces but selected at random or who had volunteered to work in the coal mining industry rather than bear arms. Everywhere you went in the surrounding countryside you were aware of a long history of coal mining. Every time we went to play football and cricket we had to climb an old spoil heap to get to the flat area of ground ('the bog') where we played and not far away there was the sloping tunnel of a drift pit or 'day 'oil' as we called it. And on the way home from school on Wakefield Road we passed another spoil heap that had been given the name Majuba (after the Battle of Majuba Hill in the First Boer War in 1881). So, as I grew up I was surrounded by coal production, a landscape full of coal mining features and coal mining families.

What strikes me forcibly is that despite the large output of books on the local coal mining industry in recent years they have mostly been about the histories of the collieries themselves or about mining disasters or photographic books, again with an emphasis on the collieries themselves. There is just one very notable exception – Dave Fordham's excellent on-going series of small books on the early development of colliery settlements on the concealed coalfield.

Mining is obviously in my genes because in one form or another I've been writing about it ever since I left school. For example, my undergraduate dissertation presented in 1959 was entitled 'Settlement Patterns and Population in a Transect East and West of Barnsley' and the last three chapters were concerned with population growth in the nineteenth and twentieth centuries and its effect on settlement patterns, i.e. it was largely concerned with the effect of the enormous expansion of coal mining on the area. I then followed this up eight years later with my MA dissertation: 'Changes in Industry, Population and Settlement on the Exposed Coalfield of South Yorkshire, 1840–1908'. The year 1908 is significant because in that year the first colliery on the concealed coalfield (Brodsworth Main) went into full production. Since then, although I've written chapters in books and articles in journals and popular magazines on such topics as child labour in mines and the development of ironstone mining, the emphasis has been on the colliery settlements and the impact of in-migration on colliery settlement growth. For example at the last count I have published seven accounts of the Welsh mining colony in Carlton and Smithies, including one in the *Clwyd Historian* and another in *Hel Achau*, the journal of the Clwyd Family History Society.

And so I thought it was time to bring all these studies together in one comprehensive volume. In the first chapter a number of critical general issues are discussed including the impact of geology on the speed and direction of colliery development, the importance of transport developments, the expansion of markets for coal and the significance of migration in peopling the new mining settlements. This is then followed by six chapters in which the different types of colliery settlement are discussed through a series of detailed case studies. The final, very short, chapter looks at the villages today and the way their appearance has changed and their functions transformed.

Acknowledgements

I would like to acknowledge the help of the following individuals and institutions in providing information and illustrations and/or for providing general help: Michael Bentley, Avril Bramhall, Tony Dodsworth, Brian Elliott, Dave Fordham, Russell Howe, Brian Marsden, Chris Sharp of *Old Barnsley* and the staff of Barnsley Discovery Centre, Rotherham Local Studies Library & Archives and Sheffield Local Studies Library. I also acknowledge permission to use extracts from out of copyright (more than 50 years from the end of the year when it was published) Ordnance Survey maps. I would particularly like to thank Eric Hill for allowing me to use his painting of the Long Row at Carlton on the front cover of the book and Steve Tye for his poem. Last but not least, I would like to thank my wife Joan for proof-reading, her many helpful suggestions, her photographs and her forbearance.

Chapter 1

General Considerations

The location, the timing of their creation and early rapid growth, their size, their morphology (i.e. their shape and design) and the geographical origins of the populations of South Yorkshire's coal mining villages were dependent on a range of factors. These were principally geology, coal mining engineering developments, transport innovation and expansion, the growth and distribution of markets for coal and coke and other by-products, changing social attitudes, including those of colliery company owners, and economic stagnation and decline in other regions throughout the country, stimulating in-migration to South Yorkshire.

Geology

The geological formation of the South Yorkshire Coalfield is relatively simple (Figure 1.1). The coal seams dip from west to east. The Lower Coal Measures of the exposed coalfield are characterised by more frequent gritstones than the Middle Coal Measures in which shales are dominant and sandstones more localised. In consequence of this, and their more westerly position up the Pennine slope, the Lower Coal Measures are more elevated. The productive Middle Coal Measures and the barren Upper Coal Measures of the exposed coalfield form country which is lower in altitude, with sandstone outcrops frequently providing well-drained settlement sites and a country in which transport developments were easier to engineer. The exposed coalfield ends and the concealed coalfield begins in the east where a band of Magnesian Limestone, a few miles wide, stretches from near Hampole in the north to near Thorpe Salvin the south. The concealed coalfield then stretches eastwards across the Humberhead Levels.

The main impact of the geology on mining development was the dip of the coal seams from west to east. In the west they outcropped at the surface and as they dipped eastwards they could at first be mined at shallow depths. The further east they dipped, the deeper any mining development had to be. There are records of coal mining on the Lower Coal Measures and the western parts of the Middle Coal Measures from medieval times, but this did not give rise to settlements in which only miners or mostly miners and their families lived. Work forces were small and the miners lived among people engaged in a range of other rural and industrial occupations. For example, as late as the 1770s, Elsecar Colliery had only five men working underground and the nearby Low Wood Colliery had only seven underground workers even though the two collieries supplied coal over a large area in South Yorkshire and neighbouring north Nottinghamshire (Jones, 1980). It

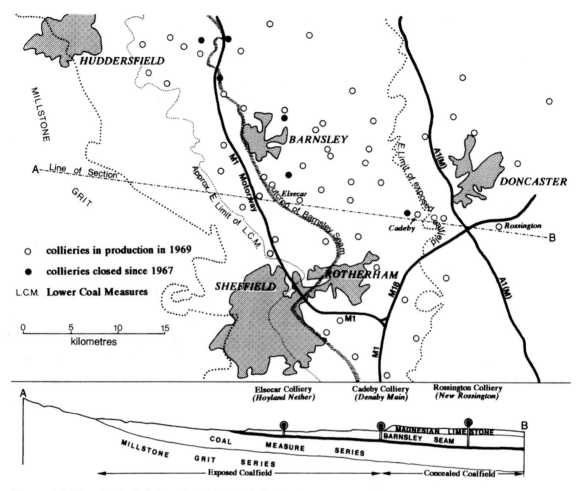

Figure 1.1 The South Yorkshire Coalfield in 1969, showing the boundary between the exposed and concealed coalfield, the eastward dip of the coal measures, the outcrop of the Barnsley Seam and the then large number and wide distribution of working collieries.

was not until the nineteenth century with quickly growing markets and improved transport that the coal mining settlement *per se* began to be created.

A considerable number of coal seams have been exploited in the South Yorkshire coalfield. Below is a brief description of the characteristics and quality of the main seams in the order in which they outcrop across the coalfield. In the west in the Lower Coal Measures are the **Halifax Hard and Soft Beds**. The Halifax Hard Bed was worked formerly in the Hazlehead district and the Soft Bed around Stocksbridge. The floors of both of these seams consist of a hard siliceous rock, ganister, which was worked from the middle of the nineteenth century as refractory material (for making furnace linings). The **Whinmoor Seam**, also found in the Lower Coal Measures, was up to four feet thick, but because of its variability was of indifferent value. The **Silkstone Seam,** which marks the beginning of the extensive Middle Coal Measures was, during the nineteenth century, second in importance only to the Barnsley Seam. The seam was of great purity and the coal was in great demand as a house and coking coal. Two Thorncliffe seams, **Thorncliffe Thick** and **Thorncliffe Thin** are present in South Yorkshire, the Thorncliffe Thin being of considerable value. The **Parkgate Seam** was up to five or six feet thick. It is a semi-anthracitic coal and was of great value in the southern part of the coalfield. **Fenton Coal** is a split seam formerly of value around Barnsley and to the south, the **Flockton Seam** was a good house coal and the **Joan and Lidgett Coals** were thin but persistent seams. The **Swallow Wood Coal** occurred over a wide area in South Yorkshire as a seam up to six feet thick and was worked as a second-class steam coal. The **Barnsley Bed** was the seam of greatest importance, exceeding in thickness and quality any other seam in the coalfield. It owes its pre-eminence partly due to the considerable thickness which it reached over a wide area (up to nine feet), but still more to the fact that it combined a soft bituminous house and coking coal with 'hard' or semi-anthracitic coal of excellent quality, well adapted for use on locomotives, steamers and for iron smelting. **Kent's Thick** was a substantial seam of indifferent quality. The **High Hazel (or Hazles) Seam** was a good seam three to four feet thick but only workable in a few places. The **Beamshaw Coal** was a good house coal. **Abdy (Winter)** and **Two Foot (Sough)** were two thin seams. **Wathwood (Meltonfield)** was a second-class house coal that covered a wide area.

Coal Mining Engineering Developments

The gentle easterly dip of these relatively thick seams and the absence of large-scale faulting enabled coal mining to be carried on from early times. The early coal workings were either in the form of shallow bell pits or adits and these proliferated at or near the outcrops of the seams. Deeper workings required advances in shaft sinking and lining, winding mechanisms for men, materials and the coal itself, safe ventilation and drainage systems and, of course, the invention of the safety lamp. Two South Yorkshire mining engineers had a great part to play in these developments. One was John Curr (1756–1823), viewer of the Duke of Norfolk's collieries in Sheffield between 1777 and 1801 and Benjamin Biram (1804–1857), superintendent of Earl Fitzwilliam's collieries at Elsecar. Curr patented flat ropes to replace single round ropes and guide rods with a 'tippler' at the surface to improve the winding of coal up the shaft and its automatic unloading. Curr also introduced what he called 'rail roads' down the collieries to transport coal from the face to the pit bottom and four-wheeled corves (coal wagons) instead of the wicker baskets of hazel pulled on sledges that had been used in the Duke's collieries before his appointment (Medlicott, 1999). Biram developed an anemometer to measure the flow of the air through mine workings and an underground fan to improve mine ventilation. An important mining engineering innovation still stands in Elsecar today (Clayton, 1995). This is the Newcomen-type engine at Elsecar built to

Figure 1.2 The Newcomen-
type pumping engine at
Elsecar.

pump water out of Earl Fitzwilliam's Elsecar New colliery (Figure 1.2). It began work in 1795 and operated continuously until 1923. It is a scheduled ancient monument.

Only when engineering developments were adequate could large-scale development take place and be maintained, accompanied by the growth of colliery settlements beside the deep collieries. But, of course, there were setbacks, the worst of these resulting in great loss of life, as at the explosion at Lundhill Colliery in 1857 where 189 men and boys perished, the explosion at the Oaks Colliery, Barnsley in 1866 when 384 died and the explosion at Swaithe Main Colliery at Worsbrough in 1875 when 143 men and boys were killed.

Transport Innovation and Expansion

Until the last years of the eighteenth century, the communications system consisted of a network of turnpike roads of varying quality, together with the navigable stretches of the main rivers, but both were inadequate. For example, Sheffield's cutlery and other light trades products destined for the Humber ports and the London and overseas markets had to be taken by road to the river port of Bawtry, then carried on the River Idle and the River Trent before reaching the Humber.

This began to change for the better in the 1760s, when canal construction began and this culminated in the 'canal mania' of 1790–94. Altogether, between 1760 and 1800, 165 canal acts were passed, so that by the end of the eighteenth century the whole country was covered by a complex system of inland waterways.

The inconvenience and slowness of the overland journey from the coalfield to Bawtry led the cutlers of Sheffield to explore the possibility of making the River Don navigable to Sheffield from Doncaster, then the head of navigation. Work began in 1726, but it proved impracticable to extend the waterway beyond Tinsley because of the number of weirs and dams and so Tinsley remained the terminus until 1819 when the Sheffield Canal opened between Tinsley and the centre of Sheffield. In the 1780s Earl Fitzwilliam built a branch canal from Greasbrough to Parkgate where it joined the Don Navigation. This canal became redundant in the 1820s and was later filled in except for a short arm to Park Gate Colliery, which was a major supplier to Park Gate Iron & Steel works. Here a new satellite settlement grew up (see Chapter 3). Parallel changes were taking place to the north of Sheffield. The Barnsley Canal was opened in 1799 to the Barnsley Basin at Old Mill and a branch canal to the Barnby Basin opened in 1802 (Glister, 1996). This canal opened up the coalfield around the town and brought about the introduction of Silkstone Coals to the London market. Five tramroads linking collieries to the Barnby Basin were included in the Parliamentary Bill for the canal. In 1804 the Dearne and Dove Canal was completed from Swinton to Barnsley, a distance of ten miles, with two-mile-long branches to Elsecar and Worsbrough, that triggered increased coal production and the expansion of settlement (Figure 1.3).

Meanwhile the country was being transformed by steam railways (Figure 1.4). In the early years of the railway era, there was anxiety in South Yorkshire lest the region should be left without up-to-date communications, and encouragement was given to all projects for bringing railways to the coalfield. However, efforts to bring the North Midland line through Sheffield failed. George Stephenson was unable to cope successfully with the steep gradients which were encountered in the vicinity of Sheffield and the line was finally taken down the easier gradients of the Rother valley to Rotherham and northwards down the Don valley as far as Swinton, then across the exposed coalfield via Darfield and Cudworth on its way to Leeds. The line was opened in 1840 and Sheffield was left five miles from the main line. A branch line was constructed from Sheffield to Rotherham in 1838 to connect with the North Midland line.

A complex network of railways was completed across the exposed coalfield over the next seventy years. There was a flurry of development by competing companies in the 1840s and

Figure 1.3 Looking south across the Worsbrough branch of the Dearne & Dove Canal towards Edmunds Main Colliery. (*Illustrated London News, 16 July, 1859*)

Figure 1.4 The railways transformed the South Yorkshire coalfield in the nineteenth century. Shown here is an example of a standard gauge railway wagon used to transport coal. (*Trevor Lodge*)

1850s and then another major development in the 1880s. The network was completed in the early 1900s. Following the opening of the Midland line, the next railway route to be completed was the Manchester, Sheffield & Lincolnshire Railway's trans-Pennine route that opened in 1845. This route came into South Yorkshire via the Woodhead tunnel and followed the Don valley into Sheffield, from where it was extended to Grimsby in 1847. A branch line from Penistone to Barnsley was opened in 1857. The South Yorkshire Railway Company formed by the Don Navigation Company, opened a route from Swinton to Doncaster in 1849 and the extended this westwards up the Dearne valley to Barnsley in 1851, with branch lines to Elsecar and through the Dove valley at Worsbrough. This route had a marked effect on the Dearne valley settlements. The same company also saw the potential of the area to the west of the Dearne valley and in 1854 opened another line from the Blackburn junction on the Sheffield to Rotherham Railway, which ran northwards to the Aldham Junction east of Barnsley on the company's Dearne valley route. On this route were the ironworks and collieries of Newton Chambers at Thorncliffe and it led to the development of Wharncliffe Silkstone and Rockingham collieries. Another Sheffield to Barnsley route was opened by the Midland Railway in 1897 via Chapeltown and the Tankersley Tunnel with a 3½ mile goods only branch to Birdwell and Pilley. Nine deep collieries were linked to this line.

A very important railway development in the last quarter of the century was the Hull & Barnsley Railway which entered South Yorkshire north of Brierley and then turned south to Cudworth. There were two important branch lines across the then rural Magnesian limestone plateau to Denaby Main (1894) and to Wath via Thurnsoe (1902). The Hull & Barnsley Railway also involved the opening of new docks in Hull, the Alexandra Docks, specially constructed for the export of coal.

The last railway to run through the heart of the exposed coalfield was the Dearne Valley Railway, sponsored by a number of mining companies in the area. It ran from Shafton in the north in a south-easterly direction near to Grimethorpe, Houghton Main and Hickleton Main collieries to Cadeby, beyond which it crossed the Don on an impressive 1,527 feet long 21-arched viaduct on its way to Black Carr West south of Doncaster. The Shafton to Cadeby section was opened between 1902 and 1908 and the section to Black Carr West in 1908. Yorkshire Main Colliery at New Edlington on the concealed coalfield lay on this route.

On the concealed coalfield, although coal mining did not begin until 1907, the first railway to enter the coalfield was the Wakefield, Pontefract & Goole Railway in 1848, running south from Knottingley in West Yorkshire to Askern Junction. More than sixty years later, Askern Main Colliery was sunk beside this railway. In 1849 the Great Northern arrived linking Doncaster with London, 160 miles to the south. This was followed in 1849 by the South Yorkshire Railway from Swinton to Doncaster which between 1856 and 1859 was extended to Thorne Waterside and the Don navigation at Keadby. This line was replaced by a new line in 1866 by the Great Central Railway. Also in 1866, the West Riding and Grimsby Railway, from Wakefield to Scunthorpe and Grimsby was opened across the concealed coalfield and Bullcroft Main and Hatfield Main collieries would later lie on this route. Another important late development linking concealed coalfield collieries was the South Yorkshire Joint Railway, completed in 1910 from Kirk Sandal Junction on the Great Central Railway south through Maltby to Dinnington and beyond to the Great Central railway at Brantcliffe west of Worksop. The last mineral railway was a joint enterprise between the Hull & Barnsley and Great Central railways. It opened in 1916 and covered 21 miles linking the Aire Junction in West Yorkshire to Braithwell Junction with short branches to Bullcroft Main, Bentley and Yorkshire Main collieries.

The Growth and Distribution of Markets for Coal and Coke

A large amount of the coal produced in the South Yorkshire coalfield was, of course, consumed within the coalfield itself. There was a large domestic demand from the population of South Yorkshire which by the end of the nineteenth century had reached 850,000. There was also a large and growing market from railways, from gasworks and from the enormous iron and steel industry within the region and beyond. Most of the deep collieries had associated coke ovens and by-product plants. By the 1950s, for instance, Manvers Main at Wath had the largest coking plant in Europe. Brickworks were also a feature of most colliery pit-top operations. From the 1870s there was also a rapid increase in the demand for coal from Europe, the latter assisted by the lowering

Figure 1.5 Smithy Wood Coking Plant. (*Chapeltown & High Green Archive*)

of tariffs on seaborne trade. Coal exports from the Yorkshire and Derbyshire coalfield via Goole, Grimsby, Immingham and Hull grew from half a million tons in 1870 to over two million tons by 1885 and over six million tons by 1911. With the building of the Hull & Barnsley railway in 1885, Hull quickly outstripped its rivals and four million tons of South Yorkshire coal were exported from Hull in 1911.

What also needs to be emphasised is that the market within South Yorkshire and beyond its boundaries was not only for coal and coke but also for the by-products of the carbonisation of coal. For example, the Smithy Wood Coking Plant, between Ecclesfield and Chapeltown, was a vital part of the Newton Chambers enterprise (Figure 1.5). Here from 1929 coal was converted into coke for the blast furnaces, and as a by-product, oil was extracted for the production of Izal, the disinfectant. The plant consisted of fifty-nine coke ovens of the most modern type when installed by Woodall- Duckham. The plant was designed to produce coke oven gas for Sheffield Gas Company, together with 5,800 tons of coke, 100 tons of ammonium sulphate, 68,000 gallons of tar and 29,600 gallons of crude benzole every week. Its operation was continuous and an oven was discharged and re-charged every twenty minutes.

Social Attitudes

The characteristic features of the coal mining communities in South Yorkshire reflect the social attitudes of the time in which they were created and developed. And these attitudes changed over time. Most but not all of the housing in the coal mining settlements in the early stages of their development was provided by the colliery owners themselves. Where this was the case the owners not only controlled who worked at their collieries but also who lived in the company-built villages. At first the housing was very basic: terraced rows of small houses without bathrooms or inside toilets, indeed in many early settlements toilet facilities had to be shared between a number of families. There were no private gardens but allotments were usually provided. As the coalfield developed and collieries increased in size and complexity an element of social control was also introduced as the houses of the families of senior officials were segregated from the rest of the labour force and were often built in a different design and size from the rest of the housing stock. This is very forcibly shown, for example, at Canklow, Denaby Main (Figure 1.6), Thurcroft and New Rossington. From the beginning of the twentieth century, the 'garden city' principle was introduced into colliery village design and so the mining settlements took on a different shape and layout. But the mine managers and colliery company directors (if they lived locally) sometimes continued to mostly reside some distance from the colliery, sometimes in pre-existing country residences.

Social control also manifested itself in the dismissal of miners and their eviction (and their families) from their cottages during disputes as at Thorncliffe (see Chapter 2) and Denaby Main (see Chapter 6). There was also often an element of 'soft paternalism' where the colliery company not only controlled who lived where but also built for the ordinary miner a type of housing that

Figure 1.6 Colliery company villas originally built for senior staff in Buckingham Road, Denaby Main.

was better than normal at the time and also provided churches, chapels, schools, community spaces and other amenities. This is best demonstrated at Elsecar but was also a feature elsewhere across the coalfield.

Migration

What will become clear is that the explosive population growth that took place in the nineteenth and early twentieth centuries, because of the expansion of the coal mining industry was stimulated by high levels of in-migration into the coal mining communities and high levels of out-migration from rural areas and other areas of economic stagnation and/or decline.

One way of making sense of all this movement is to use the **push/pull concept**. This simply states that for any individual the decision to migrate results from the interplay of two forces: pressures at the permanent place of residence (pushes) and inducements from a number of potential destinations (pulls). Examples of push factors are low wages, unemployment, political, social and religious oppression and natural disasters such as drought, famine and flood. Pull factors include employment offers and opportunities, better medical and social provision, and political and religious tolerance.

It is clear that in some cases the pushes will be of major significance, for example when unforeseen disasters occur. Two very different migrations illustrate this point. In 1857 the potato blight brought famine to rural Ireland. In 1841 the population of Ireland was 8.2 million. By 1851 the population was 6.5 million. The commissioners of the census remarked that at the normal rate of increase, the population should have been over nine million, so the real loss was about 2 ½ million people in ten years. People simply fled. And Irish-born migrants were found in almost every coal mining community in South Yorkshire in the nineteenth century. On a much smaller scale was the migration of Welsh coal miners and their families from Mostyn in the parish of Whitford on the Dee estuary in what was then Flintshire when the Mostyn Quay Colliery was flooded in 1884. When it became clear that the colliery would never re-open, the impact on the community was devastating. Two hundred men and boys who had worked at the colliery became unemployed and shopkeepers and other trades people felt the effect of the disaster. The only answer for hundreds of people was to migrate (see Chapter 4).

Many migrations take place in a series of relatively short movements often in the past from hamlet to village, to small town and finally to a large regional centre. In the nineteenth century sometimes short moves resulted from decline of domestic industry in the countryside and the concentration of employment in factories in towns or the expansion of a new industry. Take for example the case of the Dryden family who were handloom linen weavers in Brompton near Northallerton in the then North Riding of Yorkshire in the 1830s. But domestic linen manufacturing was in rapid decline and it was reported that linen weavers there were 'in great distress' because of low wages and scarcity of employment. So the Dryden family moved 20 miles further south to Knaresbrough in 1837 but found the same situation there. So they moved another 15 miles to Leeds in 1840 and by 1851 they were living in Barnsley another 20 miles more to the south. At that date the head of the family and two of his sons were handloom weavers, who worked in their cellar loomshops, and one daughter was a linen winder. But they were overtaken by events. The linen weaving industry was becoming a factory industry. By 1871 one son was a linen factory hand, and three other sons were coal miners.

In the case of coal miners there was often movement from older coal mining areas to newer ones, because of a combination of declining opportunities in the older mining areas and new and expanding opportunities in newly developed areas. This accounts for the movement of migrants from Staffordshire to South Yorkshire in the second half of the nineteenth century, a movement which continued into the twentieth century. In many cases these migrants had themselves been migrants into the Staffordshire coalfield from more rural parts of the Midlands. Whether moving from small settlements to larger settlements or simply from a declining areas to ones with new opportunities these migrants, often made several moves and were taking part in what has become known as **stepwise migration**.

There is another component to the push-pull concept. The potential migrant is confronted by one or a number of real or perceived obstacles that must be overcome before migration can take place. These may be, for example, physical (distance being the most obvious physical barrier), financial, or legal (work permit regulations, immigration quotas). What also needs to be remembered is that satisfaction with the place in which a person lives is based on first-hand experience; for other places it may be based entirely on second-hand information. If we return to the millions of people displaced by the Irish potato famine, the dilemma facing those starving, extremely poor potential migrants is very clear: where could they go and how could they finance their journey? Many made the very short journey to England but large numbers went to North America. In some cases their migration was **sponsored**. For example, Earl Fitzwilliam who owned 90,000 acres in Ireland, mostly in County Wicklow, organised a scheme for assisting poor and penniless small estate tenants. Between 1847 and 1856 he provided sea chests for family belongings, arranged for transport to the port of New Ross where hired ships were waiting to

Figure 1.7 Coal miner Robert Samuel Jones, his wife Margaret Jane and their two sons, Emrys and David, shortly after their arrival in Smithies in 1903. They had taken part in a stepwise migration from Mostyn in North Wales to Smithies via Parr in Lancashire. They were part of a chain of migration following earlier pioneer migrants from their home area to Smithies and Carlton.

takc impoverished tenants and their families to Canada. There was no force involved, all the adults volunteered to take part in the migration, which, it must be admitted, was not without self interest on the part of the earl: he was able to re-assign their tenanted plots to new tenants. Altogether he sponsored the migration of 850 families, amounting to 6,000 men, women and children. Sponsorship in the coal mining industry in South Yorkshire occurred in terms of recruiting specialist staff (e.g. pit sinkers or colliery managers), or recruiting non-union labour when strikes and/or lock-outs took place (see Chapter 2).

A distinction is sometimes made between what are termed active and passive migrants. Active migrants are the pioneers, the trail-blazers, who take the physical, financial and psychological risks, get jobs and become established at a new location. They send messages back to the former home area and they are then followed by other migrants who feel they are taking much less of a risk. These are the passive migrants. It is often, relatives, friends and neighbours who make up the flow of passive migrants and a **chain of migration** is established. This can be illustrated by the migration of the Welsh miners from Mostyn in North Wales to Carlton after the local colliery was flooded in 1884 (Figure 1.7) See Chapter 4 for further details.

An area that would be interesting to research in detail, but is beyond the scope of the present volume, is the attitude of mining migrants to the areas they have left behind for their new lives in South Yorkshire. The anecdotal evidence is mixed. For example, in his book *Oxford into the Coalfield*, Roger Dataller (Arthur Eaglestone, 1892–1980), a local writer, reported that he was told in New Edlington in 1931 that Durham miners sent their dead relatives back to Durham to be buried regardless of expense (Dataller, 1934, p.24), but in 1933 he was told that housing, unemployment and general social conditions in Staffordshire were so bad that most ex-Staffordshire residents did not want to be reminded of it again (Dataller, 1934, p. 130).

Conclusion

It is against this background of an increasing ability to reach and mine at depth a considerable number of rich coal seams and to transport the coal, coke and other by-products to markets near and far, both national and international, that mining settlements, large and small, were created and developed. And it was not just homes that were built. They were accompanied by churches and chapels, schools, community buildings and public open spaces, pubs, clubs, cinemas and sporting venues. And it was not just bricks and mortar but also people. The mining settlements were populated from every corner of Great Britain and Ireland – and beyond. For this reason each case study will consider not only the layout and design of the settlement but also aspects of its social geography, particularly the places of origin of the mining population.

The next six chapters are devoted to in-depth case studies of examples of six very different types of mining settlement in South Yorkshire, many of which survive to this day, although now there is very little sign of the collieries that were their *raison d'être*:

Chapter 2:   Small Isolated Mining Colonies on the Exposed Coalfield

Chapter 3:   Satellite Mining Villages on the Exposed Coalfield

Chapter 4:   Once Small Villages on the Exposed Coalfield expanded into Mining Communities through Infilling and Extension

Chapter 5:   Once Small Villages on the Exposed Coalfield expanded into Mining Communities mainly through Peripheral Expansion

Chapter 6:   New Mining Villages on the Exposed Coalfield

Chapter 7:   Mining Settlements on the Concealed Coalfield

The information provided does not claim to be exhaustive and those who have researched in detail individual settlements will no doubt be able to add to and modify some of the settlement histories. Space does not allow for the detailed study of every settlement and those that fall within large urban areas are not considered here, for example Handsworth and Darnall in Sheffield, Stairfoot and Hoyle Mill in Barnsley and Dalton in Rotherham. A reading list is provided at the end which may encourage enthusiasts to follow up particular lines of enquiry.

Chapter 2

Small Isolated Mining Colonies on the Exposed Coalfield

Not all mining settlements were in the form of large villages or fairly substantial satellites with a nucleated shape; some were relatively tiny or were linear, consisting of one or two long rows of housing, with possibly a church, chapel or school at one end or the other. There are five examples of small colonies lying relatively close together in the Dearne valley near Wombwell: Lundhill Row originally built to accommodate miners working at Lundhill Colliery; Concrete or Concrete Cottages consisting of eight parallel streets of diminishing length built in 1876 in a field south of the Dearne & Dove Canal, beside the Elsecar Branch railway south-east of Wombwell; Mitchell Main built just to the south of Mitchell Main Colliery; The Junction, between Wombwell and Concrete Cottages, part of which it is said was known as 'three-cornered hell'; and Broomhill about a mile to the east of Wombwell. Lundhill Row, Concrete Cottages and Mitchell Main are looked at in detail below. Another example is Long Row, built beside Wharncliffe Woodmoor 4 & 5 (New Carlton) Colliery and which is depicted in a painting by Eric Hill on the front cover of this book. There were also two very different colonies associated with the firm of Newton Chambers: the Westwood Rows at High Green built in 1870 to accommodate 'blackleg' labour after the locking out of 850 miners at their pits by Newton Chambers in 1869, and The Warren at Chapeltown that also accommodated miners working in Newton Chambers pits and most of which survives as part of a suburban outlier of the city of Sheffield. Another is the colourfully-named Klondyke between Monk Bretton and Cudworth. Woolley Colliery, the settlement not the colliery, was also a tiny colony consisting of just two terraced rows parts of which still survive.

Lundhill Row and Concrete Cottages

It is not possible to discuss the growth of these small mining colonies in the Dearne valley in isolation without considering their relationship to the growth of the town of Wombwell, because they fed off each other. Wombwell was too far away from the new collieries springing up around the town to expect everyone employed in sinking or working at the collieries, especially key personnel, to try to find accommodation for their families in the emerging town and yet the collieries were too near to Wombwell to expect any new colonies associated with them to develop into fully-fledged settlements with a wide range of services (and entertainments).

Wombwell in the 1850s was still an agricultural village perched on an outcrop of Oaks Sandstone above the flood plain of the River Dove. Within half a century it had seen enormous expansion and become a thriving town in a township that had become an urban district and whose population had increased from 1,169 in 1841, to 10,952 by 1881 and by 1901 to 17,536. By 1901 the town was populated not only by coal miners but also by business and trades people and their families. The town had been lit by gas from the town's gasworks from 1870 and by the end of the century running water was supplied to most houses from the town's waterworks. In 1886 a new parish church had been built to replace the largely medieval chapel of St Mary and there was a wide range of nonconformist places of worship. Education in the town was also well catered for and by 1900 there were three board schools with 1,550 children attending. The High Street had become a very important retailing and business area by the beginning of the twentieth century. The market place had been opened in 1875 and across the road on the south corner with Station Road stood the new Town Hall built in 1897. Along High Street and its extension to the south (Park Street) was a wide selection of businesses vying for the custom of the population of the town and the small coal mining settlements in the surrounding area (Figure 2.1). There were three banks, a succession of public houses, drapers and milliners, jewellers, pawnbrokers, newsagents, tobacconists, confectioners, greengrocers, fishmongers, hairdressers, butchers, fishing tackle dealers, cycle agents and, most imposing of all, from 1902 a new building containing Branch No. 3 of the Barnsley British Co-operative Society (boot & shoe dealer, draper and butcher in its early days).

Figure 2.1 High Street, Wombwell, *c*. 1900. (*Old Barnsley*)

And so, as the collieries were sunk in the surrounding area and coal started to be produced, small settlements grew up in their vicinity and, not far away, Wombwell responded not only by accommodating miners and their families but also by taking on the functions of a town providing an ever increasing range of services for its own population and for those settling in the new mining settlements in its immediate hinterland. Three of these are discussed below.

Lundhill Row was built as accommodation for workers at Lundhill Colliery which was opened in 1855 to take advantage of the nearby Dearne & Dove Canal and the branch line of the South Yorkshire Railway to reach its markets. This colliery was the scene of a large explosion soon after its opening with an enormous loss of life. This occurred on 19 February 1857. At the time of the disaster 220 men and boys were down the pit and 189 lost their lives. The impact on local communities was calamitous: 90 wives lost their husbands and 220 children were rendered fatherless. A second explosion took place three hours after the first explosion with a column of flame one hundred feet high. The colliery was re-opened after the disaster and continued as a separate colliery until the late 1880s when coal from the workings began to be wound to the surface at Wombwell Main Colliery.

Lundhill Row is the most primitive of the isolated mining colonies in this part of the Dearne valley. It consisted simply of one long row of brick-built cottages with shared privies (Figure 2.2).

Figure 2.2 Lundhill Row. (*Brian Elliott*)

There was no school, just a chapel and a nearby public house, the *Lundhill Tavern*. In 1901, when the inhabitants would have been working at the neighbouring Cortonwood Colliery, Wombwell Main or the Elsecar collieries, the 53 cottages were occupied by just under 300 people. Although the majority had been born in South Yorkshire, there were in-migrants from all parts of the British Isles. There were those from the neighbouring counties of Derbyshire, Lincolnshire and Nottinghamshire on the eastern side of the Pennines; from Lancashire across the Pennines and from other industrial and coal mining counties such as Durham and Staffordshire. They had also come from north and south Wales, Scotland and even from London. And they had come from the smallest of rural villages deep in the English countryside to try to earn a living in the mining bonanza of South Yorkshire. There was one person living in Lundhill Row in 1901 who had been born in Stoke Climsland in the Tamar valley in Cornwall and another who had been born in the tiny village of Redgrave in Sufffolk.

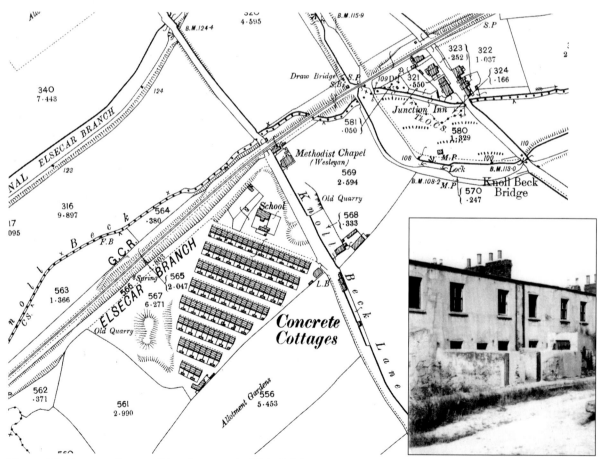

Figure 2.3 Concrete Cottages: (a) as shown on the 25-inch OS map published in 1903 and (b) inset: a rare photograph of the cottages. (*Old Barnsley*)

The scttlement called **Concrete Cottages** (or just **Concrete** as it was called at the time of the 1901 census) was built in a field south of the Dearne & Dove Canal beside the Elsecar Branch Railway. It was sometimes referred to as New Wombwell or Little Palestine (because the houses had flat roofs, it is said). It had been established in 1876 by the Cortonwood Colliery Company following the sinking of Cortonwood Colliery the previous year. It was composed of eight unnamed streets, varying in length from nineteen to four houses, 106 homes altogether (Figure 2.3). Each street faced north-east so that the view from the windows of most of the cottages was into the backyards of other cottages. And as the name of the settlement implies the cottages were indeed made of concrete: the walls, the roofs and even the spouts. There were two rooms on the ground floor, a living room which contained a black leaded fireplace, and a kitchen with a Yorkshire range fireplace, a 'copper' (a boiler used for heating water and washing clothes) and a stoneware sink with a cold water tap. Below the kitchen was a cellar used for storing coal and foodstuffs. Upstairs were three bedrooms, one large room and two small rooms. The large bedroom had a fireplace. In the early years the living room and kitchen were lit with gas but candles had to be used upstairs. Each cottage had its own private backyard with earth closets. At the northern end of the settlement, beside Knoll Beck Lane, stood a small (two-room) school and a Wesleyan chapel (the 'Tin Chapel'). There were small shops where the shopkeepers operated from their front rooms, a tiny post office and a fish and chip shop. Allotment gardens were provided in the field next to the village. The cottages were occupied until 1958.

In this tiny purpose-built mining settlement in 1901 lived 580 men, women and children. And as in all the other mining settlements that had sprouted up across the exposed coalfield during the nineteenth century many were in-migrants from all parts of the country and beyond. They had been born in neighbouring Cheshire, Derbyshire and Lincolnshire, from Lancashire, Durham and Staffordshire and from further away from London and Kent. There were also people who had been born in Flintshire and Anglesey in north Wales and from Ireland. And they had come from the most rural parts of England – from Norfolk, Suffolk and Cambridgeshire. Most surprising of all there was one person who had been born in the 'US of America, British Subject'.

The area once covered by Lundhill Row, Concrete Cottages and Lundhill and Cortonwood collieries has now been landscaped and contains a dual carriageway, suburban housing, a lake, a golf course and retail park.

Mitchell Main

The short-lived isolated colony at Mitchell Main was associated with Mitchell Main Colliery (or as it was originally known Mitchell's Main Colliery). This colliery, located between the Dearne & Dove Canal and the South Yorkshire railway (by 1904 the Great Central Railway), just half a mile north-west of the centre of Wombwell, began to be sunk in 1871 and the Barnsley seam was reached in 1873 at 307 yards. From the early 1900s the seams below the Barnsley seam (Parkgate,

Fenton, Silkstone and Swallow Wood) were exploited. The colliery changed hands in 1883 and the Mitchell Main Colliery Company retained ownership until nationalisation in 1947.

A small settlement, roughly rectangular in shape, was built immediately to the south of the colliery mainly between the canal and Barnsley Road (Figure 2.4). It comprised four streets of cottages: one in the west with cottages on one side of Barnsley Road; another with cottages along one side on Bradberry Balk Lane in the south; a long street in the north called Myers Street with

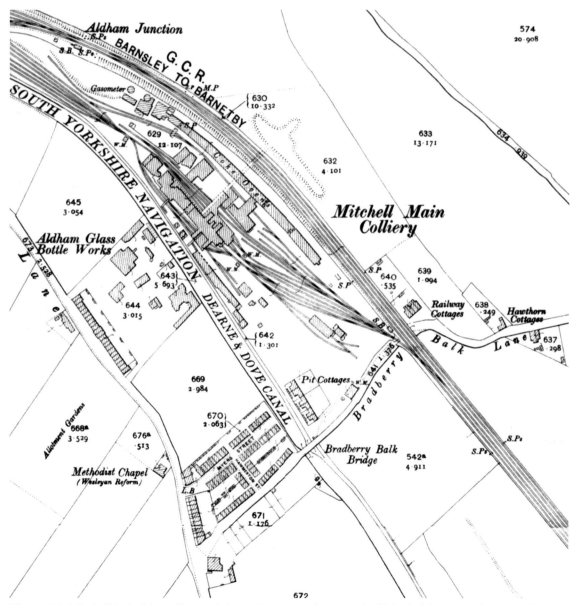

Figure 2.4 Mitchell Main (the colliery and the settlement) as shown on the 25-inch OS map published in 1906.

cottages on both sides; and through the middle Hammerton Street cutting through Myers Street to Bradberry Balk Lane. There was also a substantial house just outside the colony on the corner of Barnsley Road and Bradberry Balk Lane. Across the canal was a short row of six cottages called Pit Cottages and further to the north-east across the railway were four cottages called Railway Cottages. There was also a single row of about a couple of a dozen cottages (that still survive) on the Barnsley Road to the north beside the Aldham Glass Bottle Works, which stood between the cottages and Mitchell Main Colliery. There was a Wesleyan chapel but no school. Myers Street and Hammerton Street were still marked on the Ordnance Survey Street Atlas published in 1996 but are now gone. The chapel still stands.

An analysis of the 1901 census returns for this small settlement, which was recorded under the name Mitchell Terrace, is most revealing. In the main settlement (i.e. excluding the Railway Cottages and the long row opposite Aldham Glassworks), there were 89 cottages containing a population of 434. These cottages were the homes of 150 working men and boys of whom 123 (82 per cent) worked at the colliery. Nineteen men and boys (13 per cent) worked at the glassworks. There were six widows heading households, one of whom was a shopkeeper selling sweets and another two who were said to be lodging house keepers. One male head of household was a railway worker, one was retired and all the others not working at the colliery or in the glassworks were offering services – two were wagonnette proprietors, one was a barber, one was a grocer, one was a butcher and one was a 'yeast hawker', i.e. a 'barm man'. What is not surprising is that of the 150 working men and boys living at Mitchell Main in 1901, only three of the 83 fathers and 21 of their 52 sons and one of the 15 boarders had been born in Wombwell. Fifty-five of the working men and boys had been born in the rest of South Yorkshire and a further 22 had been born elsewhere in Yorkshire. There were also migrants from neighbouring counties, the West Midlands and the more distant counties of Suffolk and Cornwall. There were also four migrants from Wales (from Flintshire, Denbighshire and Glamorgan) and seven from Ireland. Significantly, the next household recorded by the enumerator after leaving Mitchell Main was on a canal boat called *Annie Lee*!

The Long Row at Carlton

The Long Row or to use its formal name, Carlton Terrace, was located about half a mile from the centre of the village of Carlton across Shaw Bridge between the Barnsley Canal and the railway, beside what was at first called Carlton Main Colliery and later Wharncliffe Woodmoor 4 & 5 or New Carlton to distinguish it from Wharncliffe Woodmoor 1, 2 & 3 (Old Carlton) to the west of the village. The colliery was leased to the Yorkshire & Derbyshire Coal & Iron Company. The first sod was cut by the Earl of Wharncliffe of Wortley Hall, under whose estate the coal was going to be exploited, on 12 November 1873. But sinking did not commence until the following year. The nine feet thick Barnsley seam was reached in 1876. The colliery was closed between 1910 and 1924 when it was taken over by Wharncliffe Woodmoor Colliery Company who operated the colliery until nationalisation in 1947. The colliery closed in July 1970.

Within just a year or two of the opening of the colliery the Yorkshire & Derbyshire Coal & Iron Company had built Carlton Terrace beside the colliery (Figure 2.5). At first it consisted of sixty brick and twelve stone cottages and by 1890 another twelve cottages had been added. The original weekly rents were four shillings and sixpence (22½ pence) for a stone cottage and four shillings and threepence for a brick cottage. In 1901 there were 81 occupied residences on the row including a shop and a working men's club. Small as they were, some were very crowded with one household consisting of 14 people and another of 12. Seventeen households contained boarders. The total population was 492. What is not surprising is how many people were incomers. Of the 173 working men and boys all but six (which included the shopkeeper and the club steward) worked at the colliery including those in senior positions such as a colliery underviewer, a coal inspector and eight pit deputies down to coal hewers, banksmen and colliery labourers. But only 18 (10 per cent) of these 173 workers had been born in Carlton and they were mostly the sons of migrants. Seventy-four (43 per cent) of these working men and boys had been born in the rest of Yorkshire, overwhelmingly (65 or 38 per cent) from just a few miles away in South Yorkshire. Most of the other migrants (30) were from the West Midlands of whom 22 were from Staffordshire. There were also migrants from the most unlikely places in rural England: there was a coal hewer who had been born in the tiny village of Redgrave in Suffolk and

Figure 2.5 The Long Row at Carlton.

a colliery deputy whose birthplace was Cornwall. There were also two migrants from Scotland, two from Ireland and four from south Wales but none from north Wales, even though Carlton had a thriving and growing community from North Wales. The migrants from north Wales all worked at Old Carlton pit and lived in other parts of Carlton and in Smithies (see Chapter 4).

Wharncliffe Woodmoor 4 & 5 closed in July 1970, and soon afterwards the colliery headgear and associated colliery buildings and Long Row were all demolished. The 130-acre area was contoured and landscaped, the canal diverted, the road network improved and Lyons Bakery covering eight acres (and said to be the biggest cake factory in the world!) was built there.

The Westwood Rows

Taking a country walk through the wooded Thorncliffe valley and in and around the former Tankersley deer park, now largely converted into a golf course, about halfway between Barnsley and Sheffield, it is difficult to realise that you are in the vicinity of a former settlement connected to one of the most celebrated labour disputes of the nineteenth century (Jones, 1993). The dispute in question rivalled, in its physical confrontation between locked-out miners and the forces of

Figure 2.6 An aerial view of Westwood Rows shortly before their demolition towards the end of the 1960s. (*Chapeltown & High Green Archive*)

law and order, the more recent national strike of 1984. After the dispute was over, the employer involved, Newton Chambers & Company, described it as 'the most determined contest between capital and labour which is to be found in the mining history of this or any other country'. They went on to say that the action of the miners created 'not only indignation but astonishment in this and other countries'.

The settlement concerned was called the Westwood Rows (Figure 2.6). This isolated settlement was built at the end of the 1860s to house 'blackleg' miners recruited by Newton Chambers and it was demolished towards the end of the 1960s. It had come and gone within a hundred years. The site was subsequently open-cast mined and then landscaped and seeded to form part of Westwood Country Park. Today no sign remains of a settlement that for most of its existence housed more than 300 men, women and children.

The dispute that gave rise to the building of the Westwood Rows lasted for seventeenth months from 24 March 1869 to 17 August 1870. There had been a dispute only three years earlier that had lasted for nine months and this was followed by an uneasy two years in which there were two more disputes, but all that had gone before paled into insignificance when compared to the bitterness, resentment and physical disturbance associated with the 1869–70 dispute, the worst violence talking place in and about the Westwood Rows.

Briefly the dispute stemmed from the decision of Newton Chambers to reduce wages by 7.5 per cent and their refusal to negotiate with the Miners' Union. Workers were to continue to be employed provided they agreed to abide by the rules and by-laws of the Company's collieries which involved them in, among other things, negotiating individually over wages and working an eight hour day when required to do so. It was essentially then, an attempt to eliminate collective bargaining, and the workers at the company's collieries – Thorncliffe Drift, Tankersley, Norfolk, Newbiggin and Staindrop – were given a month's notice to cease work or to submit to the company's demands. On 24 March 1869, 850 men and boys were locked out, although several hundred remained at work.

The evidence – which includes evidence from the miners' union, company records, personal diaries, newspaper reports, letters to local and national newspapers, court proceedings and the 1871 census - is particularly rich and interesting. The diaries are particularly interesting. One surviving diary is that of George Dawson, head of the ironworks, a figure seen by the striking miners as a major stumbling block in the way of a swift and fair settlement. Another is that of William Nesbitt, a man from north-east England, who had been appointed foreman engineer in the fitting shops at Newton Chambers in December 1868, only a few months before the dispute began. The early entries record a sense of personal danger of someone very close to the action and later ones of a 'fly on the wall' watching the action unfold.

The evidence reveals a situation in which there was constant tension, anxiety and foreboding. The employer stood firm and attempted to replace the striking miners with blackleg labour from other parts of the region and from other coalfields. The strikers, not surprisingly, tried to persuade the blacklegs to return home. They succeeded in this to some extent, but inevitably the supply of blackleg labour increased and this was combated by outbreaks of violent behaviour aimed at intimidating the newcomers. This, in turn, led to police and military reinforcements being brought to the area, and inevitably the tension increased. The immediate surroundings of Newton Chambers' Thorncliffe Works must have taken on the appearance of a town under siege.

William Nesbitt recorded the beginning of the dispute in his diary in a very matter of fact way:

March 24th Finished 3 ft pulley for hay cutting machine for company's farm, being 5 days in the lathe.

Mr Thomas Chambers youngest daughter was married today to Mr Hawett of Nottingham and the affair came off very quietly.

All the coalminers of the Thorncliffe Colliery Co'y came out on strike.

By the beginning of April he noted that several policemen had arrived at Thorncliffe 'to protect property and the men that have started work at the pits, against the men who are on strike.' The next day (2 April) he noted that two blacklegs who had started work at Thorncliffe Drift Pit 'were guarded to work by policemen'. A month into the strike and with no sign of a settlement, Nesbitt noted that orders had been given 'for all tenants to clear out of Thorncliffe Cottages as he (Mr John Chambers, the partner principally concerned with the running of the collieries) wanted the houses for his blacksheep. The Thorncliffe Cottages (or Thorncliffe Rows as they are better known) lay much nearer the ironworks than Westwood Rows would be, in the valley of the Blackburn Brook south of Thorncliffe Drift Colliery. They had been built during a previous dispute in 1866 to accommodate non-union labour. Despite the fact that some newcomers were being induced to return home before taking up residence and work at Thorncliffe (Nesbitt recorded blacklegs being met at Chapeltown station and having their return passages paid for them), the eviction of the striking miners and their families from Thorncliffe Rows and the installation there of blackleg miners and their families led to the first major outbreak of violent behaviour. William Nesbitt, who was himself living in Thorncliffe Rows at the time, wrote that a body of striking miners, about 200 in number, came at 10 o'clock at night and 'Drove the policemen out and broke all the windows in five houses'. The policemen 'ran in all directions, some hiding themselves in the water closets'.

Throughout the rest of 1869 there were outbreaks of violence of varying degrees of severity and periods of mounting tension when it was believed that a major disturbance was about to occur, these being accompanied by reports of 'many strangers being in the district'. Potential blackleg miners continued to be met at the local railway stations by angry crowds of strikers. By 23 October it was reported in the *Sheffield and Rotherham Independent* that representatives of Newton Chambers were seeking the assistance of the army in the form of a permanent garrison because the neighbourhood was 'in a state of constant terror' and an attack was expected on the homes of the working miners. In November 1869 the miners' union admitted that as many as a hundred 'blacksheep' were working in the firm's collieries. Leading members of the firm also began to receive threatening letters. For example the following letter was received by Mr Arthur Marshall Chambers:

> *Mr Chambers 1870 Sir. Prepare to meet thy God, as I insist on thee been a dead man before long. if thou means to keep us this winter. We are determined not to let you see the end of it. if thou means to let us clam & starve. we mean to have it out of you you bugger as thy Days are numbered. so prepare to meet thy God.*
> *Yours truly one who wishes you in hell fire.*

Then on 7 January 1870, a crowd of strikers attacked Tankersley pit, broke windows, smashed lamps and pushed several corves (coal wagons) down the shaft. The engine 'tenter' (i.e. the person who looked after the engine) alerted the local population by a long and continuous blowing of the pit buzzer, and as the rioters broke into the engine house he hid himself under the floorboards. This was followed on Friday 21 January at seven o'clock in the morning by an attack on the fronts and the backs of the new cottages at Westwood Rows. The crowd of attackers, variously estimated at between 300 and 1500 men were 'armed with pistols, some with bludgeons, the heads of which bristled with spikes, some with picks' according to the *Sheffield and Rotherham Independent*. The cottages were defended by a force of ten policemen who were overwhelmed, though not before dispatching a messenger to Barnsley for reinforcements. In the ensuing mayhem windows were smashed, doors and furniture demolished, houses looted and an unsuccessful attempt was made to set fire to the cottages by burning clothing, bedclothes and broken furniture. Police reinforcements then arrived from Barnsley and set about the crowd with cutlasses to which the miners replied with their bludgeons. Thankfully no one was killed. Twenty-three men were eventually sent for trial at York assizes, eleven receiving sentences of imprisonment, three of them for five years.

Following these disturbances soldiers, about one hundred in all, were quartered in the Workmen's Hall at Mortomley Lane End and at Tankersley Farm for six months, and an uneasy peace returned to the area. The dispute lasted another seven months, ending on 17 August. Wages were reduced, former workmen had to re-apply on an individual basis and there were no vacancies at Thorncliffe Drift Pit, presumably all places being already filled by non-union men, local and migrant. The concessions made by the company were relatively minor. Subscriptions to the accident fund were to be optional rather than compulsory, all Saturday working was reduced to half a day (it had previously been one half day Saturday per fortnight) and although fortnightly pay remained, money could be advanced on a weekly basis if earned.

So who were the blacklegs who were recruited by the company and installed in Westwood Rows? We know that the company employed an agent to recruit miners in other coalfield areas and that the miners' union tried to combat this by distributing leaflets in the same areas, putting their side of the argument and asking miners to stay away from from Thorncliffe. One of these, for example, claimed that the company was giving a false name to the collieries concerned 'for the express purpose of deceiving you, and, thereby, leading you into the **Black Trap**.'

Some light can be shed on the origins of the non-union miners by analysing the enumerators' returns of the 1871 census for the Westwood Rows, the census having taken place just seven months after the end of the dispute. The returns show that 47 of the fifty cottages were occupied with a total population of 327. Twenty-two of the 47 households had lodgers. Altogether there were 125 males in employment whose ages ranged from 10 to 69 years of age. Ninety per-cent were employed in collieries, overwhelmingly described as coal miner, miner, collier or pit labourer, but also including three trappers, two pony drivers, two engine drivers, two engine tenters, two deputies, a carpenter, a blacksmith, an assistant underground steward and an underground viewer. The evidence provided of the birthplaces of the residents suggests that the majority were families or single men from other areas who had been recruited during the dispute. That they were recent migrants is proved by the fact that in some families there is a young child born locally in contrast to his or her older siblings born elsewhere. For example, in the Jervis family there were eight children, seven of whom were born in Derbyshire, including the next to the youngest, four-years old Charles, who was born in Ilkeston, but the youngest child, Arthur, who was two, was born in Tankersley (i.e. in the Westwood Rows). Similarly in the Grealy family, of their four children, two were born in Derbyshire, the next to youngest, Michael, who was three, was born in County Durham, but their youngest daughter, Mary, who was one year old was born in Tankersley. Both parents were born in Ireland.

Of the 125 employed males, 35 were born in South Yorkshire, mostly in Tankersley and Ecclesfield parishes; the next biggest group (22) were born in Derbyshire and seem to have been recruited in the Chesterfield and Ilkeston areas; there were 18 from Leicestershire, all born in and around the mining settlements of Moira and Donisthorpe in the north of the county and from Overseal just across the county boundary in Derbyshire. There was another substantial group (14) who had been born in Ireland, although the birthplaces of their wives and children show that they had been resident in south Lancashire, north Derbyshire, Durham and the Black Country before coming to the Westwood Rows. Most of the remainder of the employed male migrants originated from mining areas around the country including Lancashire, Durham, Northumberland, Shropshire, south Wales and Scotland.

The Warren

The Warren has the distinction of being one of the three of the isolated colonies discussed in this chapter that survives to this day, but now it is simply a semi-isolated suburban strip. Warren was a residential colony for local workers developed rather late bearing in mind its proximity to

Newton Chambers' Thorncliffe Ironworks and related collieries. The first Six-inch Ordnance Survey map, surveyed in 1850 shows just four buildings at the western end on the south side of Warren Lane and a public house at the east end on the south side of the lane. Warren Lane is so called because the lane ran along the former southern boundary of Tankersley deer park, that part of the park just north of the lane was named The Warren because it was a part of the park where the red deer hinds gave birth to and looked after their young fawns. The park belonged to Earl Fitzwilliam of Wentworth Woodhouse but the land to the south of the lane belonged to the Duke of Norfolk, hence the name of the public house at the end of the lane, the *Norfolk Arms*.

In 1881 there were 732 people in 154 households living on Warren Lane. There were 227 employed persons of whom 105 (46 per cent) worked in collieries. The rest were in a wide variety of occupations including a slater, a toll bar 'tenter', a schoolmistress, and a bootmaker but most were employed at the Thorncliffe Ironworks in a variety of capacities. Interestingly, one of the inhabitants of Warren in 1881 was William Vernon who has two claims to fame. First, he was the engine 'tenter' at Tankersley pit in 1870 when it was attacked by rioters. He blew the buzzer to warn troops that rioting was taking place (then hid under the floorboards). Secondly, he ran

Figure 2.7 *The Miners' Arms*, Warren Lane.

the first co-operative store in the district from his own cottage on Warren Lane until the society erected a purpose-built shop.

In 1881 just over 60 per cent of the employed men and boys living on the Warren were migrants, i.e. they had been born outside Ecclesfield parish in which Warren Lane was located. The biggest group of worker migrants (37 per cent) were from the rest of Yorkshire, mostly short and medium distance migrants but there were also long distance migrants from the East Riding (Hull) and the North Riding (Scarborough). The next biggest group of migrants (16 per cent) were from the neighbouring counties of Derbyshire, Lancashire, Lincolnshire and Nottinghamshire, but, as in all the other South Yorkshire mining communities in the second half of the nineteenth century there was a sprinkling of long distance migrants in this case with representatives from Somerset, Devon and Wiltshire in south-west England, from Northumberland in the north of England and one head of household born in Ireland.

By the time of the publication of the 25-Inch Ordnance Survey map published in 1903 there were buildings all the way along the south side of Warren Lane as far as the modern Thorncliffe Road that links the A616 (Stocksbridge by-pass) with the Thorncliffe industrial estate. This consisted mostly of housing in the form of terraced rows, including at the western end some short rows of back-to-back housing. It also included two more public houses, the *Thorncliffe Arms* and the *Miners' Arms* (Figure 2.7), a Wesleyan chapel and Sunday school built in 1859 (which had originally operated also as a day school) and across White Lane at the eastern end of the settlement, Warren School, opened in 1900 with places for 100 infants and 268 older children.

Today the remaining terraced houses on the south side of Warren Lane are accompanied by twentieth century-built bungalows and semi-detached and detached housing on the north side.

Klondyke

This small industrial colony lay on Burton Lane between Monk Bretton and Cudworth. At the beginning of the twentieth century it consisted of two short rows of terraced houses on Burton Lane itself and three short terraces leading off to the north at right angles called Faith Terrace, Hope Terrace and Charity Terrace. So the settlement as a whole formed a small square (Figure 2.8). Within walking distance lay Monk Bretton Colliery to the south-west, a brick works to the east, the Midland Bleach works to the north-east and railways almost encircled it. There were, therefore, employment opportunities in almost every direction.

In 1901 the population of Klondyke was 253, living in 43 households. Household size varied from two to 14 and ten of the households contained boarders or visitors including a female evangelist preacher from Liverpool. There were 92 employed men and boys living in Klondyke in 1901. Of these, 72 (78 per cent) worked in a colliery, from deputy down to trammer and pony driver. Six men or boys worked on the railways, four at the brickworks and three at the bleach

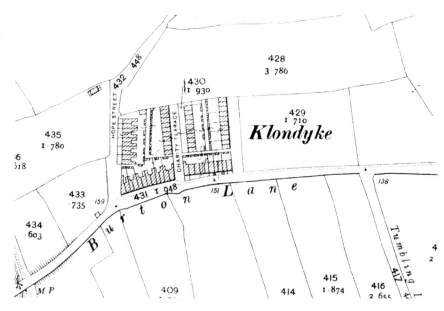

Figure 2.8 Klondyke as shown on the 25-inch OS map published in 1906.

works. One person, an elderly man born in Ireland, worked as a farm labourer. Another two worked as grocers, presumably from a small shop in a front parlour.

The birthplaces of these employed men and boys were as varied as in all the other mining villages in South Yorkshire at the time. Forty-one (45 per cent) were from South Yorkshire but only five had been born in Monk Bretton parish where Klondyke was located and only one from neighbouring Cudworth. Nine had been born in other places in Yorkshire and nine had been born in Staffordshire. There were then small numbers from Derbyshire (six), Lancashire (six) and Ireland (six). Among the other interesting birthplaces were four from the Forest of Dean in Gloucestershire, which was also a coal mining area, and one each from Walsham in Suffolk, and Rotherfield in Sussex, both distant rural villages. One man who worked as a colliery horsekeeper was born in Scotland and another who worked at the brick works was from Whitechapel in the East End of London. But perhaps the most surprising migrant living in Klondyke in 1901 was a fourteen-year old trapper who had been born in Iowa in the mid-west of the USA! His father, who had been born in Royston must have crossed the Atlantic in both directions. If the boy had been told that the family was leaving the USA to go to Klondyke, he may have believed he was going to Klondyke in the Yukon in north-west Canada to mine gold not to a small settlement in South Yorkshire to mine coal!

The settlement still retained the name Klondyke in the 1950s but later became officially known as West Green. It still survives to this day in part.

Woolley Colliery

The colliery 'village' of Woolley Colliery lay just below Woolley Edge above the Dearne valley about half a mile north of Darton and a mile and half south of the estate village of Woolley. It lay right beside the Barnsley branch of the Yorkshire & Lancashire Railway that had arrived in this part of South Yorkshire in 1850. Small-scale mining had a long history in the area exploiting the seams that outcropped on the hillside above the River Dearne. There is a record of coal mining in the manor of Woolley as early as 1301–02. But some of the earliest pits dug here were not for coal but for trapping wolves. It was recorded about 1257 on two occasions that there were wolf pits in the wooded hills around Woolley and, of course, the place-name Woolley means a 'woodland clearing frequented by wolves'.

Modern mining in the area began in March 1854 under the ownership of the Woolley Coal Company. The early history of Woolley Colliery was the subject of detailed research by John Goodchild some 30 years ago (Goodchild, 1986). At first shallow drift mines (adits) were worked at various places below Woolley Edge and there was a shaft mine at Woolley Warren House and then in 1869 shafts were sunk in Wheatley Wood about three-quarters of a mile to the north-east of the site of the colliery village of Woolley Colliery. At this site the Barnsley and Beamshaw seams were exploited (locals used to call this pit the 'Beamshaw pit'). There was a mineral railway from Wheatley Wood to the Barnsley branch of the Yorkshire & Lancashire railway. The company had financial difficulties and was sold in 1867 to a new company called the Woolley Coal Company Ltd and then again in 1873. In 1894 the colliery was purchased by Fountain & Burnley Ltd who already owned North Gawber Colliery. The Fountains of North Gawber Colliery were the surviving sons of George Fountain (died 1871) of whom only Joseph Fountain was alive in 1894 (he died in 1904). George Burnley, was the husband of the Fountain brothers' sister, Ellen. He died just a few months after agreeing the purchase of Woolley Colliery. On Joseph's death in 1902, his sister Annie Christine Fountain, who married Sir William Sutherland in 1921, became the principal shareholder. The couple lived at Birthwaite Hall north of Kexbrough and within site of the winding gear of Woolley Colliery. Between 1910 and 1912 two shafts were sunk at the site of the modern Woolley Colliery that eventually exploited seven seams. Fountain & Burnley Ltd continued to own Woolley Colliery until nationalisation in 1947. The colliery was eventually closed in December 1987.

The colliery settlement of Woolley Colliery, which first came into existence in the late 1860s, was located right beside what became the site of the modern colliery (Figure 2.9). The colliery, its coke ovens and the colliery slag heaps eventually stretched north-westwards beside the railway and the 'village' lay immediately to the east of the colliery. Originally the village consisted of two stone rows, (the Old Rows) of terraced houses. These rows were demolished in two stages between the late 1950s and the beginning of the 1970s.

An analysis of the 1901 census returns for the old stone rows is most revealing. They show that in that year there were 25 households living in the Top Row and 29 in the Low Row. The number

Figure 2.9 Looking from Woolley Colliery north–eastwards towards Low Row, showing the close proximity of the residential colony to the colliery. (*Old Barnsley*)

of people in a household varied between one (a 66-year old, female, colliery clerk) and twelve. A number of the households contained boarders as well as family members. The total population of the two rows was 277.

There were 91 working men and boys living in the two stone rows in 1901 of whom 88 (96.7 per cent) were employed at the colliery. These ranged from a colliery under manager, eight deputies, two corporals (men in charge of a certain district in the colliery under a deputy) to hewers, screenmen and pony drivers. The three men not employed at the colliery were two stone quarry men and a mason's labourer.

As might be expected in a relatively new settlement, only six of the 91 employed men and boys had been born locally (either in Woolley or Woolley Colliery). Most of the rest of the working population were short distance migrants from the rest of South Yorkshire (22 or 24 per cent), for example Gawber, Darton and Barnsley) and from neighbouring West Yorkshire (45 or 49 per cent). The West Yorkshire migrants came both from areas immediately to the north, stretching from Wakefield, Rothwell and Leeds and from the woollen cloth manufacturing area to the north-west (e.g. Huddersfield, the Dewsbury area and in and around Halifax). Unlike most other South Yorkshire mining villages on the exposed coalfield at that time, there was only one migrant from Staffordshire and there were only seven long distance migrants including one from the village of

Wimpole in Cambridgeshire, two from Sudbury in Suffolk, one from Hitchen on the outskirts of London in Hertfordshire, one from Miele in Ireland and another from Perth in Scotland. The step-wise migration concept (see Chapter 1) is well illustrated by one of the migrant families whose head, a colliery engine fitter, was born in Sudbury in Suffolk. His wife was from Staffordshire, his elder son (a colliery engine driver) had been born in Durham and his younger son, who also worked at Woolley Colliery, had been born in Staincross.

The two rows were extended eastwards in 1913, this time in brick and the names Top Row and Low Row continued to be used for the new additions. These brick cottages survive to the present day. The gap between the two rows became Bluebell Road on both sides of which, to the east of Top Row and Low Row, a few council houses were constructed. In the 1930s a miners' institute was built and there was a small general store and a 'chip 'oil'. The only road out of the village was Woolley Colliery Road leading down the valley side into Darton. There was a footpath (now Bluebell Road) leading into Husband Wood and another path leading north and east to the Mission Church and school and beyond into Windhill and Wheatley woods. The school did not have any electric lighting as late as the 1940s. But what is forgotten is that although the miners and their families often lived in cramped conditions close to the colliery, in which the men and boys worked, they also often lived, as in this case, close to the countryside and could enjoy, within a short walking distance, bluebell woods in spring, hedgerows full of elderberries, sloes and blackberries in the autumn and skylarks singing overhead.

Following the closure of the colliery, the site of the colliery and its slag heaps were opencast and landscaped and are now the site of an up-market housing development called Woolley Grange. As you drive into the approach road (The Grange) from Woolley Edge Lane with its flower-bedecked entrance it feels as if you are on the drive to a large private country residence. Instead you are met with the gleaming exteriors of new detached villas, semi-detached houses and three-storey townhouses built on a series of winding drives, courts and closes. All this is in West Yorkshire. And then you cross the road into South Yorkshire and suddenly you come upon the Top Row and the Low Row and Bluebell Road, survivors from another era, another world. The Miners' Institute, the school and the church have all gone. The houses in the two rows, that became Coal Board houses on nationalisation, are now mainly privately owned and modernised.

Chapter 3

Satellite Mining Settlements on the Exposed Coalfield

A feature of the development of the exposed coalfield was not only the building of isolated small settlements, usually near the pithead, the expansion of existing rural villages into medium-sized mining villages or even small towns and the development of completely new mining villages, but also the growth of satellite settlements either near to but separate from an existing settlement or merging with an existing settlement but retaining its own identity. Hoyland is unusual in that it was ringed by satellite settlements. With the others, it is simply the twinning of an old village with a new settlement as in the case of Rawmarsh with Parkgate and Wales with Kiveton Park, or two new settlements as in the case of Worsbrough village with Worsbrough Dale and Worsbrough Bridge.

Satellites at Hoyland Nether: Elsecar, Hoyland Common and Platts Common

Nowhere is the growth of satellite mining settlements better exemplified than around the settlement of Hoyland Nether (in its early days in the extensive ecclesiastical parish of Wath upon Dearne) and just across its boundary in neighbouring Wombwell township. Much has been written about coal mining in the Hoyland area (e.g. Ward [1963]; Clayton [1973]; Mee [1975] and Medlicott [1998]). This is hardly surprising so intensively was the exposed coalfield in this area exploited. There are records of at least 20 collieries that operated within four miles (six kilometres) of Hoyland Nether village in the last 250 years.

Although we know that small pits were being worked near the outcrop of the Barnsley Seam near the western edge of Hoyland Nether township in the seventeenth century (Clayton, 1973), the first detailed records of coal mining date from the eighteenth century. These relate to Low Wood Colliery and Elsecar Colliery. Low Wood was in Wentworth and Brampton Bierlow townships and Elsecar was just inside Hoyland township, less than a mile to the north-west. The first record of Low Wood Colliery is 1723. Elsecar was first mentioned in 1750. Both collieries worked the Barnsley Seam near its outcrop, the pits sunk for Elsecar Colliery being no more than 16 yards (15 metres) deep. The seam, as already noted, was nine feet thick. From the early 1750s both collieries were under the Wentworth estate's direct control. These were small collieries with, in the 1760s and early 1770s, only five men working under ground at Elsecar Colliery and seven at Low Wood. Both collieries were distant from navigable water, the coal had to be transported in horse-drawn wagons and yet in the second half of the eighteenth century they had surprisingly large market areas. This can be gauged from debt lists for the two collieries that survive for the 1762–88 period (Jones, 1980). There were 263 individual entries for the two collieries. If it is assumed that people living in one area were no more likely to incur bad debts than people in another area then the lists are very instructive. The markets for Elsecar coal were more local than those for Low Wood coal. They stretched north-eastwards into an area where there were no rival collieries, the route crossing the River Dearne towards the Magnesian Limestone escarpment and the lowlands beyond. The market for Low Wood coal stretched in the same direction but also included lowland areas further east extending into Nottinghamshire and Lincolnshire. Transport for Elsecar coal was all by horse-drawn wagon but Low Wood coal was transported by cart five miles (eight kilometres) to the estate wharf on the River Don at Kilnhurst where it could be transported on the canalised river to markets on the lower Don and Trent.

The presence of the thick Barnsley Seam and other seams, principally the Silkstone Seam and the Parkgate Seam, that could be reached from deep pits, together with improving transport links by canal and railway, and the expanding ironworks on the estate, all contributed to the vast expansion of the coal mining industry in and around the Hoyland area from the late eighteenth century onwards.

The Act of Parliament for constructing the Dearne & Dove Canal, along nine miles of the Dearne valley with cuts to Elsecar and Worsbrough, received parliamentary sanction in 1793 and the Elsecar branch was completed by 1796 as far as Cobcar Ings. By 1799 it had been extended to Elsecar where a new colliery, Elsecar New Colliery was sunk. There were three shafts at the new colliery, two coal-winding shafts and one pumping shaft. The pumping shaft was powered by a Newcomen-type engine which has survived to the present day virtually intact and *in situ* and is a Scheduled Ancient Monument. Not only was there a new colliery at Elsecar, but the workings at the old Elsecar Colliery were extended and by 1850 there were three Elsecar collieries: Elsecar High Colliery (the Old Elsecar Colliery), Elsecar Mid Colliery (formerly Elsecar, New Colliery with a new shaft at Jump) and Elsecar Low Colliery at Hemingfield, just inside Wombwell township. Both the Mid Colliery and the shaft of the New Colliery at Jump were connected by inclined planes to the canal. In 1851 all three of these collieries were connected to the railway system when a branch line of the Dearne valley route of the South Yorkshire Railway was built to a goods station at Elsecar. They were superseded in 1853 by the sinking of a new colliery, Simon Wood Colliery, whose shaft reached the Barnsley seam at 93 yards. This colliery was in production for almost half a century before closing in 1903. It was superseded by Elsecar Main colliery in 1908, designed initially to exploit the Parkgate Seam at 344 yards. Elsecar Main Colliery closed in 1983.

All the collieries mentioned so far were worked directly on behalf of the heads of the Wentworth estate. But they also leased mining rights to other companies. One of these was called Vizard's Colliery at Platts Common which came into operation in the early 1840s. This colliery was deepened and enlarged in 1876 and re-named the Hoyland Silkstone Colliery. It worked the Silkstone, Thorncliffe, Parkgate and Flockton seams. Coke was also made at the colliery.

It was linked to both the railway and the canal. It closed in 1928 by which time it had been acquired by Newton Chambers & Co. This firm had leased from the Wentworth estate the mineral rights just one and a half miles (two kilometres) to the south-west of Platts Common and opened Rockingham Colliery in 1875 to work the Silkstone and Parkgate seams. Like Hoyland Silkstone, Rockingham had a large number of coke ovens, 170 in all, erected in 1883, which were the main source of the oil by-products of coke making that were converted into the firm's famous disinfectant, Izal. From 1930, after the closure of the coke ovens, until 1965, an overhead ropeway four and a half miles (seven kilometres) long, carried the coal from Rockingham Colliery to the coking plant at Smithy Wood. The colliery closed in 1979. Just outside the boundaries of Hoyland Nether in neighbouring Tankersley parish were two other collieries: Tankersley Colliery, rented from the Wentworth estate by Netwton Chambers, and Wharncliffe Silkstone on land owned by the Wortley family (Earl of Wharncliffe) of Wortley Hall.

What all this colliery development and employment opportunities, stretching from the eighteenth century through the nineteenth century and into the second half of the twentieth century, led to, was a population explosion and related settlement expansion in existing settlements and the creation of completely new settlements. Hoyland Nether, the main settlement within the township continued to grow as the collieries identified above together with the Elsecar and Milton ironworks were developed. Elsecar grew from being a a small hamlet around Elsecar Green into a fully fledged mining satellite, and Hoyland Common was a completely new substantial satellite settlement and Lower Hemingfield, Jump and Platts Common were smaller satellites. Elsecar, Hoyland Common and Platts Common are discussed below.

At **Elsecar**, the Fitzwilliams created an estate industrial village which survives largely intact to this day, a testament to the high quality of the housing provided. The oldest surviving working men's houses at Elsecar are the fifteen stone cottages that make up Old Row which date from about 1795. The ten cottages on Station Row were built in about 1800, probably based on designs by John Carr, the York architect, who was employed on various schemes at that time by the 4th Earl Fitzwilliam. The largest row at Elsecar is Reform Row, consisting of 28 cottages constructed in 1837 (Figure 3.1). At the time of the 1851 census, all the heads of household, except for a few widows, were coal miners. The two attractive rows that make up Cobcar Terrace were built about 1860. In 1845 the mines commissioner, Seymour Tremenheere, described in some detail the housing provided for the miners at Elsecar. He said their houses were 'of a class superior in size and arrangement and in the conveniences attached, to those belonging to the working classes'. He went to say that 'Those at Elsecar consist of four rooms and a pantry, a small back court, ash-pit, a pig-sty and garden'. 'The gardens' he said 'were cultivated with much care'. He said that the village presented 'a remarkable contrast with the degrading neglect of cleanliness in person, house and habits, exhibited in so many of the colliery villages of Scotland' (Tremenheere, 1845). Besides the housing, Elsecar was also provided with Holy Trinity church in 1843, at the expense of the 5th Earl Fitzwilliam, and the neighbouring school was built in 1852 to replace an

Figure 3.1 Reform Row, Elsecar.

earlier school. The village had street lighting from 1857 and a market hall was opened in 1870. In 1853 even a miners' lodging house was opened that accommodated 22 single men and contained the first indoor bath in Elsecar!

In 1771 when William Fairbank surveyed Hoyland for the 2nd Marquis of Rockingham, a settlement at **Hoyland Common** did not exist (Figure 3.2). There were small holdings at Hoyland Lane End to the east, but Hoyland Common was just that, a common, covering 210 acres (85 hectares) (Jones, 2000). By 1851 a new settlement had been created beside the Wakefield to Sheffield turnpike road which ran in a south-easterly direction along the western edge of the common. In that year the population of Hoyland Common was 195. Of the 71 employed males living there, 39 were miners of whom 34 were ironstone miners. In 1854 Wharncliffe Silkstone Colliery was opened in Tankersley parish little more than a mile to the west of Hoyland Common. This had an immediate impact on the settlement, a Barnsley newspaper reporting in 1859 that 'the village of Hoyland Common seems to be improving with something like the speed observable

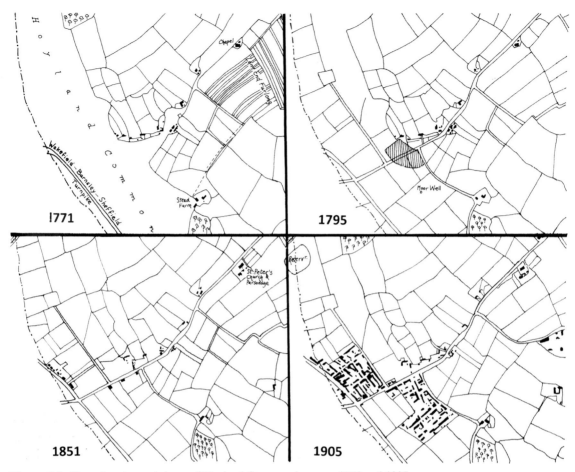

Figure 3.2 Changing size and shape of Hoyland Common between 1771 and 1905.

in American towns. Building operations are being carried on very fast and it seems as if it would soon grow into the dimensions of a town'. So densely populated had this satellite settlement become, that in 1876 a board school was erected on Sheffield Road, and according to Kelly's Directory in 1889 had a regular attendance of 417 pupils. The miners at Wharncliffe Silkstone Colliery established their trade union branch headquarters at the *Hare & Hounds Inn* at Hoyland Common, opposite the board school, where it remained until the colliery closed in 1967. Hoyland Common has now merged with Hoyland village, Upper Hoyland, Platts Common and Elsecar, and by 2001 they had a combined population of more than 15,000.

The Wentworth-Fitzwilliams not only provided employment as the collieries were established and expanded, but also home comforts and health care. They not only built houses, churches and schools for their workers, they erected estate almshouses, gave pensions to widows and employed doctors to look after the health of their employees. Their benevolent attitude to their workers is well exemplified by their stance with regard to the St Thomas's Day tradition in the nineteenth century. This was on the 21 December, the winter solstice, the shortest day and the longest night of the year. On that day, also called Thomassing Day, Mumping Day, Gooding Day and Corning Day, poor people begged money and provisions for Christmas. St Thomas's Day in the nineteenth century was institutionalised on the South Yorkshire Wentworth estate by successive earls Fitzwilliam. There are very full records of the custom throughout the first half of the nineteenth century. For example, in 1841 just over 1,000 servants and employees (except those in the mansion who had separate arrangements) received a gift They had to be regular employees not those doing occasional jobs. In the 1840s everyone got sixpence and a quantity of beef. In 1841 the beef distributed amounted to 439 stones (2788 kg). Everyone had to turn up personally and names were ticked off lists drawn up by heads of departments. In 1841 the lists included 631 coal miners (181 at Elsecar New Colliery, 188 at Elsecar Old Colliery, 126 at Parkgate Colliery, 54 at Stubbin Colliery and 55 at Strafford Main), and 24 ironstone miners (these were maintenance staff, the miners themselves being regarded as self-employed). St Thomas's Day and succeeding days must have been times of plenty in those households where the husband and several sons were all Fitzwilliam estate workers. The same list of employees was used in the following March on Collop Monday, which along with Shove Tuesday was traditionally a day of games, dancing and feasts to consume the food forbidden in Lent. On Collop Monday the outdoor employees of Earl Fitzwilliam were given a quantity of beef and bacon.

Until 1795 **Platts Common** was exactly what its name suggests, an area of common land on the north-eastern boundary of Hoyland Nether township. In 1795 the common was enclosed into a number of fields with two roads running across it, one towards the hamlet of Blacker and the other towards Wombwell Wood. Then in the early 1840s a small colliery was sunk on its southern edge. This was Vizard's Colliery already noted above. At first the settlement that grew up next to the colliery was very small. In 1851 it had a population of only 65 which included 23 working men and boys. Only thirteen of the 23 were employed at the colliery and these included a mine agent, an engineer, a weighman, a fitter, a fireman and a banksman. Interestingly four men were living in what was called the 'coal pit cabin'.

Platts Common remained a very small satellite of Hoyland Nether until the 1870s. Then the colliery was leased in 1873 to the Hoyland Silkstone Coal & Coke Company Ltd, the colliery was re-named the Hoyland Silkstone Colliery and three deep shafts were sunk to mine the Silkstone, Thorncliffe, Parkgate and Flockton seams. Before 1877 coal was carried down to the canal at Elsecar on an inclined plane, the coal wagons being attached to a steel cable worked by a steam engine at the top of the incline. Then in 1877 a mile-long branch railway line was constructed that linked the colliery to the South Yorkshire Railway to the north-west just inside Tankersley parish. In 1898 1,260 men and boys worked underground. The colliery was acquired by Newton Chambers in 1925 and as noted above it was closed in 1928. After closure one of the three shafts continued in use as a man-riding and ventilation shaft for the nearby Rockingham Colliery.

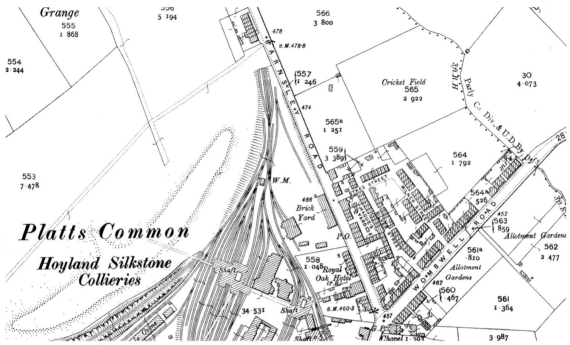

Figure 3.3 Platts Common as shown on the 25-inch OS map published in 1905.

By the beginning of the twentieth century a well established mining colony had grown up next to Hoyland Silkstone Colliery. The colliery, its coke ovens, brickyard and coal tip occupied a large area to the west of Barnsley Road and the settlement of Platts Common occupied the land immediately to the east in and around the triangle formed by the junction of Barnsley Road and Wombwell Road (Figure 3.3). By this time the settlement not only contained the cottages occupied by miners and their families but also a chapel, the *Royal Oak Hotel*, allotments and a cricket field.

Immediately across the road from the brickyard was Sykes Street and to the south of it was Hague's Yard. In 1901 there were seven cottages in Hague's Yard and eleven cottages on Sykes Street (one was unoccupied). Altogether the total population of these two areas was 79. In Hague's Yard, three of the heads of household were widows; the other four were all hewers at the colliery. On Sykes Street ten of the eleven heads of household were coal miners; the other one was a widow. Of the fourteen men and boys who worked as coal miners, six had been born in Platts Common or elsewhere in Hoyland, others were from other places in South Yorkshire (Cudworth, High Green, Higham, Sheffield, Thorpe Hesley) and West Yorkshire (Wakefield) but there were a number who were medium distance migrants (e.g., from Derbyshire, Nottinghamshire and Worcestershire) or long distance migrants (e.g., from Wootton in Oxfordshire, the Forest of Dean in Gloucestershire and from Denbighshire in north Wales). There was also a coke oven labourer living as a boarder on Sykes Street who had been born in Ireland.

With the closure of Hoyland Silkstone Colliery in 1928 and the nearby Rockingham Colliery in 1979 things changed radically. In 1973, the Hoyland local historian Arthur Clayton wrote

Now the older part of the little village of Platts Common, which grew up in the shadow of the giant headgears has been demolished. It has been replaced by a village of pleasant houses set in spacious surroundings. The old inclined railway site is also covered for the most part by new houses, while on large areas that were waste heaps, or muck stacks as the collier always called them, there are several clean, modern factories (Clayton, p.75).

Today Platts Common is a modern suburban settlement with an adjoining industrial estate. There is no obvious sign of its mining past.

Worsbrough village and its satellites Worsbrough Dale and Worsbrough Bridge

Both of these settlements are satellites of Worsbrough (originally spelled Worsborough) village which lies in the former Worsbrough Park south of the River Dove, dominated by the seventeenth century Worsbrough Hall and the medieval parish church, and physically little changed by the industrialisation in the local area and surrounding region which caused such a population explosion and settlement expansion. To the north of the River Dove, the settlement pattern before industrialisation consisted of dispersed farmsteads and the country homes of the local gentry and successful businessmen such as Marrow House, Darley Cliff, Darley Hall and Swaithe House. For example, Marrow House was the birthplace of Edith Turner, mother of the eighteenth-century poet Alexander Pope and Darley Cliff was the home during the first two decades of the nineteenth century of Charles Bowns, agent to Earl Fitzwilliam of Wentworth Woodhouse.

In 1804 'to great rejoicing' a two mile long branch canal was opened from the Dearne & Dove Canal to the Worsbrough Basin which gave access to the Don Navigation and therefore to markets in Sheffield, down the Humber to London and beyond. Then in 1852 the Worsbrough Branch of the South Yorkshire Railway, closely following the route of the canal came through the Dove valley giving access to markets on both sides of the Pennines.

These transport developments immediately sparked the creation of collieries near to the canal and the railway at Worsbrough Dale. There was Bell Ing Colliery at Worsbrough Bridge canal terminus, Lob Wood and Darley Main collieries to the west of High Street at Worsbrough Dale and Edmunds Main Colliery (opened in 1853) across the River Dove on the south side of Worsbrough Dale. Two of these collieries were the sites of underground explosions: at Darley Main Colliery in 1849 when 75 men and boys were killed and at Edmunds Main Colliery in 1862 when 59 miners lost their lives. Another colliery, Swaithe Main Colliery, north of the canal and railway, employed many Worsbrough Dale and Worsbrough Bridge inhabitants and this was also the scene of an underground explosion in 1875 that killed 143 miners. Yet another colliery,

Worsbrough Park Colliery, was established in Worsbrough Park but was soon succeeded in 1876 by the much bigger Barrow Colliery, so-called because it was the property of the Barrow Haematite Steel Company of Barrow in Furness, attracted to colliery investment at Worsbrough because of the quality of the coking coal. The company even leased Worsbrough Hall and used it as offices and accommodation for the colliery manager and agent. After nationalisation the NCB purchased it from the Edmunds family and used it as offices. They sold it in 1964. Barrow Colliery, which in the twentieth century, amalgamated with Barnsley Main and Monk Bretton collieries, closed as recently as 1991. In the nineteenth century other industries were also attracted to canal/railway-side locations including an ironworks, a steelworks, a glassworks, a gunpowder factory, saw mills and boat building yards.

The impact of these transport developments and the establishment of collieries and manufacturing industries on population levels and settlement creation and expansion was enormous. From the early years of the nineteenth century the area, except for Worsbrough village, underwent a profound change. In 1801 the population of Worsbrough township (which also included Rockley and Birdwell) was 879. Fifty years later in 1851 it had grown to 4, 277 and by the end of the nineteenth century it stood at more than 10,000. At first, settlement expansion was largely unplanned and small scale in the form of a succession of small terraced rows and groups of cottages stretching along the Dove valley for almost a mile from Worsbrough Bridge in the west to Lewden in the east. To the north of this east-west linear residential development was, by the beginning of the twentieth century, another more village-like settlement stretching north-westwards along what had become Worsbrough Dale High Street from the Mitchell Memorial Hall (erected in 1880) in the south to St Thomas' church (built in 1859) in the north and beyond to the junction with Park Road (later Sheffield Road).

Contrasting with the piecemeal development of Worsbrough Dale and that part of Worsbrough Bridge next to the river, canal and railway, was the planned residential development at Worsbrough Bridge along what was then Park Road (later Sheffield Road). There a planned settlement was laid out by the Barrow Haematite Steel Company consisting of six streets running away north-westwards at right angles from Park Road and four running away south-eastwards. Every street name was a male forename: Arthur, Henry, William, Thomas, Robert and Edmund on one side and James, John, George and Charles on the other. On the main road itself was a school, a chapel, a police station and shops including, inevitably, a branch of the Barnsley British Co-operative Society. Surrounding this planned development on the north, west and east were extensive allotment gardens (Figure 3.4).

Inevitably, the opening of the Barrow Colliery in 1876 attracted over the years migrants to the Worsbrough area, many of them occupying houses in the newly established satellite village at Worsbrough Bridge. This is reflected in the returns of the 1901 census, a quarter of a century after the opening of the colliery. On one street, Charles Street, there were 41 households with a total population of 248. Two houses were occupied just by a miner and his wife but one house

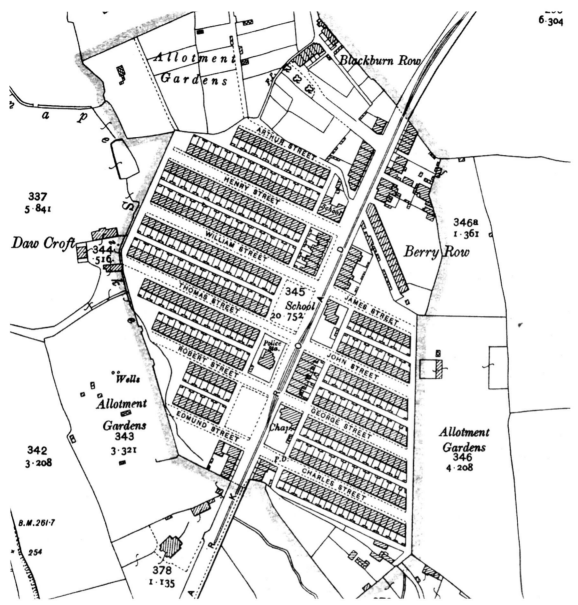

Figure 3.4 The planned settlement at Worsbrough Bridge as shown on the 25-inch OS map published in 1906.

contained 10 people, two houses held 11 people and one held 12. In the 12-person household besides the father, who worked in the colliery as a hewer, four of his sons were also miners, one a hewer like his father and the other three pony drivers. Nine households also contained boarders. Altogether there were 102 employed men and boys living on Charles Street and of these 91 were colliery workers. The other 11 included five who worked in a local iron works, a brick layer, a shop assistant, two bootmakers (one of whom also ran a sub-post office) and a shoemaker.

The employed men and boys living on Charles Street had been born in 16 different English counties from Cornwall and Kent in the south to Cumberland and Durham in the north. There were also six Irish-born miners, one from Flintshire in north Wales and another from Monmouthshire in south Wales. A quarter of these men and boys had been born in Worsbrough itself and another quarter had been born in places in the rest of South Yorkshire including large urban areas like Barnsley, Rotherham and Sheffield but also smaller places like Penistone, Thurgoland and Cawthorne and Mexborough and Wadworth further east. As usual there were migrants who had been born in the most unlikely places. One miner had been born in Tunbridge Wells in Kent, another migrant working at the colliery coke ovens had been born in Land's End in Cornwall and the bootmaker/sub-post master and his son, a shoemaker, had both been born in Godmanchester, a small town in Huntingdonshire. The question naturally arises, were there any migrants who appeared to have come from Barrow in Furness in north Lancashire, the home of the owners of Barrow Colliery? There were fifteen miners living on Charles Street in 1901 who had been born in Lancashire, including one from Barrow in Furness itself and two from neighbouring Cumberland, including a bricklayer from Whitcham, only nine miles from Barrow.

By 1902 the tramway system from Barnsley had reached the southern end of the High Street at Worsbrough Dale and the southern part of Park Road at Worsbrough Bridge. These transport developments marked the beginning of a slow change for the villages in this part of the Dove valley from industrial to suburban settlements.

Rawmarsh and its satellite Parkgate

Rawmarsh and Parkgate lie just a couple of miles north of Rotherham town centre and now constitute part of the continuous built-up area of the town. Today Parkgate in the south, merges with its northerly neighbour Rawmarsh which expanded a great deal during the twentieth century as a residential suburb and now their combined population exceeds 18,000.

The early history of the two settlements could not be more different. Rawmarsh is an ancient settlement, appearing in the Domesday Book in 1086 as *Rodesmesc* meaning 'red marsh'. This does not apply to the site of the village itself which lies at about 78 metres above sea level but to the land in the surrounding parish which to the east extends into the flood plain of the River Don. In 1811 it was already a large village with a population of 1,110 which had grown to 1,259 by 1821. Even at that date besides agriculture, there were a number of short-lived small coal pits to the south-east of the village in the direction of Aldwarke Hall and to the west in Greasbrough where the Fitzwilliams of Wentworth Woodhouse owned nearly 2,000 acres of land and were important industrial entrepreneurs. In complete contrast, the only settlement at Parkgate, which was not recorded for first time until 1559, appears to have been buildings associated with an entrance to the grounds of Aldwarke Hall to the east beside the River Don.

It was the development of new transport arteries, first canals and then railways, that transformed the local economy and eventually the settlement pattern. The first canal development took place in the early 1780s when the Greasbrough Canal was constructed by Wentworth Woodhouse estate. This canal linked the estate with the Don which had been made navigable to Aldwarke in 1733, Rotherham in 1740 and Tinsley in 1751. It finally terminated at Sheffield in 1819. Access to navigable water enabled coal from the Fitzwilliam collieries to reach markets in Sheffield in one direction and the Humber ports in the other direction. The Greasbrough Canal ran for about one and a half miles from Cinder Bridge just to the east of Greasbrough where lime kilns were constructed. Waggonways ran from their Greasbrough Colliery (formerly called the Bassingthorpe Colliery) to Cinder Bridge. The canal became redundant in the 1820s and was later filled in except for a short arm to Park Gate Colliery. Then came the railways. In 1840 the London-Midland-Scottish Railway ran down the Don valley just to the east of Rawmarsh and Parkgate, followed in 1871 by the London-North-Eastern Railway. But what gave rise to the creation of an industrial settlement at Parkgate was the decision of the Fitzwilliam estate to lease land under favourable conditions to two metal-working businesses that would consume local coal. One was under partners Sanderson and Watson that became the Park Gate Iron Works and then Park Gate Iron and Steel Works and the other run by William Oxley who made Swedish iron into steel. The first blast furnace came into operation at Park Gate Iron works in 1839. Its early prosperity was based on the production of rails for the rapidly expanding rail network but later armour plate was a major product. The plate for Brunel's steamship the *Great Eastern* launched in 1858 was made there. The works were demolished in 1976.

Besides Park Gate Colliery, which was to become a major supplier of coke to the Parkgate Iron & Steel Works, the Wentworth estate also operated collieries at Stubbin to supply Parkgate Iron & Steel Works and Park Gate Forge. The early twentieth century survivor was Top Stubbin Colliery that dated from about 1870. It worked the Barnsley Seam but reserves were becoming exhausted by the early years of the twentieth century and the 7th Earl Fitzwilliam decided to open a new colliery to work the six feet thick Parkgate Seam and later also the Silkstone Seam. The first sods of No 1 shaft of the New Stubbin Colliery were removed by Lord Milton, the earl's two-year old son in 1913, work on the shafts commenced in 1915 and coal was wound up the shaft for the first time in 1919. The colliery closed in 1978. Just to the east of what was to become the industrial village of Parkgate, Aldwarke Main Colliery, owned by Sheffield steel giant, John Brown & Co Ltd, came into production from 1865 and worked until 1961. Across the River Don, less than a mile and half to the east of Rawmarsh-Parkgate, near Thrybergh, John Brown also owned the long-established Roundwood Colliery which operated until 1931 and Silverwood Colliery which came into production in 1905 and did not close until 1991. And to the south was Carr House Colliery which was also acquired by John Brown. It is not surprising then that with the rapid industrial expansion in and around Rawmarsh and Parkgate that Rawmarsh would expand southwards towards Parkgate and that a new settlement might emerge next to the iron, (and

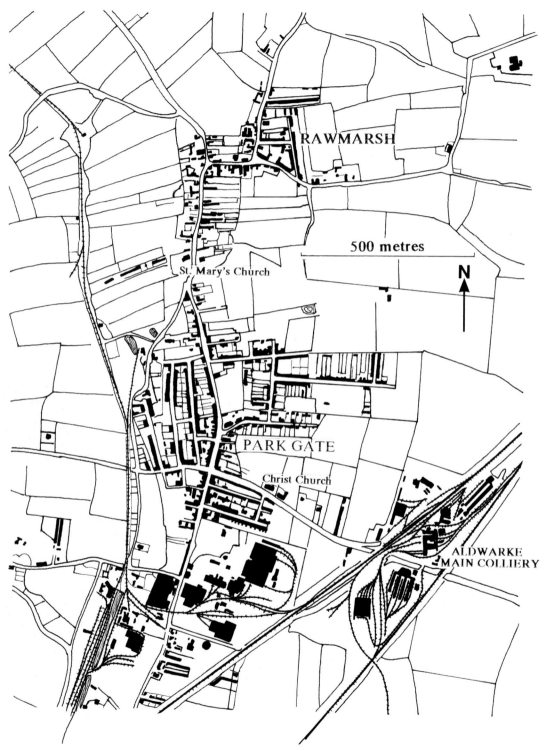

Figure 3.5 Rawmarsh and its industrial satellite, Parkgate, based on the 1896 Six-inch OS map.

later iron and steel) works and Aldwarke Colliery. And that is exactly what happened. Rawmarsh became a large mining village (population 14,547 in 1901) and a new satellite settlement, where the men and boys were employed in the ironworks and the neighbouring collieries, grew up at Parkgate (Figure 3.5). Parkgate's population had grown to 3,807 by 1871 and to 8,067 by 1901.

The morphology of the new settlement at Parkgate was and remains quite simple. Running south to north through the settlement is Broad Street. Just beyond Hollybush Road, north of the junction with Greasbrough Road running off to the west and Aldwarke Road running off the east, it becomes Rawmarsh Hill, at the top of which just, before St Mary's church, Parkgate merges with Rawmarsh. By the middle of the nineteenth century there were just a few rows of cottages near the ironworks together with Park Gate House just to the south of Aldwarke Road where Charles Stoddart, later Sir Charles Stoddart, secretary and then general manager of the ironworks lived from the 1850s until sometime in 1870s. By the end of the century the rows of cottages had multiplied enormously with new streets running off at right angles to the east of Broad Street (Figure 3.6) and Rawmarsh Hill and parallel with it behind the top end of Broad Street and Rawmarsh Hill. Christ Church, the new Anglican church was built on Aldwarke Road in 1867 on the western edge of the rapidly growing village but the vicarage was on Greasbrough

Figure 3.6 Broad Street, Parkgate, in the early twentieth century. On the left at the junction of Broad Street and Wancop Street, a load of coal has been delivered. (*Old Barnsley*)

Road on the western edge of the village next to the open agricultural countryside stretching towards Wentworth park. According to a study of Parkgate undertaken by Anthony Dodsworth (Dodsworth, 1995), many of the streets were not company houses as they were in many new industrial settlements, but appear to be the result of investment by small speculative builders (e.g. Lloyd Street by John Lloyd a railway wagon builder and France's Row by Amos France a stonemason) and according to George Royston who wrote a book about the history of Park Gate Iron steel Company (Royston, n.d.) by the miners and ironworks employees themselves through self-help societies. It is believed that the houses on Hollybush Street, Aldwarke Road and Hall Street were built in this way.

In his 1995 study of Parkgate, Dodsworth analysed the population statistics of the censuses of 1871, 1881 and 1891 for one particular street. This was Hall Street, a row of 39 terraced houses immediately to the south of Aldwarke Road. The population of this single street grew from 224 in 1871 to 253 in 1891. In 1871 only 38 of the inhabitants had been born in Parkgate, not one of these being a head of household. Half the population had been born in the rest of Yorkshire, but there were also significant numbers born in Staffordshire (37), Nottinghamshire (16), Derbyshire (11) and two families from Norfolk. Over the twenty-year period between 1871 and 1891 the numbers living on Hall Street employed in coal mining increased significantly from 12 in 1871 to 42 in 1881 and 39 in 1891. In the same twenty-year period the number of inhabitants living in Hall Street who worked in the ironworks dropped from 25 to 18.

This mixing of colliery and iron and steel works employees, both locally born and in-migrants, was typical of this rapidly growing industrial satellite in which the housing had not been built by the owners of the collieries and the iron and steelworks. This can be exemplified by an analysis of the 1901 census returns for Lloyd Street where the housing had been built by a speculative builder in the 1870s. There were 69 houses on this street, where 125 employed men and boys lived in 1901 either as the heads of families, sons living at home or as boarders. Forty-six (37 per cent) were employed in the collieries and 28 (22 per cent) were iron and steel works workers. The rest were in a wide variety of occupations from brick maker, stonemason and yeast merchant to journeyman tailor, piano teacher and mineral water manufacturer. It is also clear if this street is typical, that Parkgate was becoming a much more settled community. Even when the father or both parents were migrants, their children, including grown-up children living at home, were often Parkgate- or Rawmarsh-born or from surrounding areas in South Yorkshire (55 per cent altogether). But as elsewhere in Parkgate some of the adults had been born in distant parts, often in very small country villages: for example, Hempton in Norfolk, Hexham in Northumberland and Whitchurch in Hampshire.

Detailed accounts of life in Rawmarsh and Parkgate when they were industrial villages have been written by Roger Dataller and Gwennie Peacock. Roger Dataller, the pen-name of Arthur Archibald Eaglestone (1892–1980), published his *From a Pitman's Notebook* in the 1920s (Dataller,1925) which is in the form of a long series of literary sketches of pit life, some amusing others deadly serious, yet others very evocative, based on his seven years of working as a young man as an underground timekeeper at New Stubbin Colliery. In later life he also wrote an unpublished autobiography, *A Yorkshire Lad*, which is available in manuscript form in the Archives and Local Studies section of Rotherham Central Library. The autobiography contains detailed atmospheric descriptions of his early life living in Lloyd Street, Parkgate (his father was one of two brothers who lived on the street and who were mineral water manufacturers).

A detailed account of staying in Rawmarsh with a mining family more than sixty years ago was written by a New Zealand woman between 1939–1940 when she travelled by sea and overland to visit her relatives in Rawmarsh. The writer was Gwennie Peacock, who at the time she wrote her diary was in her very early thirties (Figure 3.7). She carried a typewriter everywhere she went and finished up writing a diary that covered just eighteen months but added up to 375,000 words and after her death it was delivered to her relatives in Rawmarsh in a brown paper parcel in 2003! An edited version has recently been published (Dodsworth, 2014).

En route to England, she listened to Mussolini haranguing a crowd in Rome and was told in Germany that before long everyone in England would be speaking German (it was 1939). When she eventually crossed the Channel she travelled all over the country including trips to Scotland and Ireland, but most of her time in Britain was spent in South Yorkshire. As she stepped off the train

Figure 3.7 Gwennie Peacock (left) the New Zealand diarist. (*Tony Dodsworth*)

in Rotherham she was greeted by 'Welcome lass!' One of her early local trips out was to Netherfield Lane, Parkgate where her grandfather and grandmother had lived and where her mother had been brought up. Her grandfather had worked at Silverwood Colliery. And what must be remembered is that she was from Auckland in the North Island of New Zealand. Everything was new to her, everything was an adventure. She'd never had Yorkshire pudding with loads of gravy as a starter, never had fish and chips for supper every night, never kissed an uncle in his 'pit muck', never heard all those dialect words and expressions like *duck* (faggot), *mashin tea*, *snap* (workman's meal), *snicket* and *weshin pots* and never lived in a mining village with its Working Men's Club and allotments or been down a coal pit (yes, they smuggled her down Aldwarke Colliery!).

Today the original steelworks has disappeared, all the local collieries have gone, Rawmarsh is now a large residential suburb of Rotherham, and Parkgate is best known as the site of an out-of-town shopping centre. But there is still a steel plant at Aldwarke, just to the east of Parkgate between the railway and the River Don, erected by the owners of Park Gate Iron & Steel Works in the 1960s, and at the time of writing owned by Tata Steel.

Wales and its satellite Kiveton Park

Anyone looking at the 25-inch Ordnance Survey map showing the villages of Wales and Kiveton Park in the extreme south of the West Riding of Yorkshire, near the border with Derbyshire published in 1902, would believe, at first glance, that here are two very different villages. On the one hand there is what appears to be a traditional, agricultural village, Wales, with its parish church and manor house set amongst its fields whose shapes in many instances betray their ancient origins. On the other hand, there is Kiveton Park, a relatively new, purpose-built colliery settlement, located beside a busy railway line, overlooked by colliery headgear, and with a Primitive Methodist chapel but no Anglican church. The truth lies somewhere between these two extremes.

Wales was first recorded in 1002 and was also recorded in the Domesday Book of 1086. Wales is from the Anglo-Saxon word *Walas* meaning 'The Welshmen', indicating the presence here of a Celtic settlement when the Anglo-Saxons penetrated the area in the seventh century. The layout of the village of Wales at the beginning of the twentieth century was linear. Although the centre of the village lies at a crossroads, almost all of the village by 1901 had grown out in mostly two directions, north and south of the road junction, for nearly a mile altogether from Wales Court in the north to the cemetery in the south. Dominating the village architecturally, as it had done for centuries, was St John the Baptist's church. This Norman church, constructed of attractive stone rubble, of varying proportions up to boulder-size, and with a Perpendicular-style west tower, had been enlarged in 1897.

There is no stream or river running through or near the village and, therefore, the village water supply before the introduction of piped water came from wells. Nineteen wells and 14 pumps are shown on the 1902 OS map in and around the village. The village at that time had a smithy where farm horses would have been shod and a surviving pinfold, a walled enclosure where stray cattle and sheep would in the past have been impounded, only to be released on payment of a fine at the manorial court. The identity of two of the three major landowners in and about the village is perfectly clear from the names of the two public houses, the *Leeds Arms* (now the *Duke of Leeds*) whose namesake bought the manor of Wales about 1775 and the *Lord Conyers Arms*, the lady of the manor in 1901 being Baroness Conyers, whose ancestor married the 5th Duke of Leeds in 1773. The third major landowning family in Wales, the Colton-Foxes, lived at Wales Court in 1901, with the trappings of a minor country family: three indoor servants and three resident gardeners, one living in the grounds in the 'bothy' and two with their families in 'The Dairy'.

Centuries of rural calm in the village of Wales must have been shattered in the late eighteenth century by the building of the 46-mile long Chesterfield Canal from Chesterfield in north Derbyshire to West Stockwith on the Trent in north Nottinghamshire. The canal was the work of the pioneering engineer, James Brindley, and was completed in 1777. The projected route was blocked by a ridge, and in order to cross this the Norwood Tunnel had to be constructed. The tunnel was 2,880 yards (2,633 metres) long and approached by 13 sets of locks on the western side and 22 on the eastern side. The canal carried coal, iron, limestone, bricks, sand and timber but its most famous cargo was the stone to re-build the Houses of Parliament (between 1841–44) which was transported on the canal from the vicinity of Kiveton Park, having been brought on carts from the quarry at North Anston, 1½ miles to the north-east. The Norwood Tunnel partially collapsed in 1907 and the canal went into decline. Large sections of the canal have now been faithfully and beautifully restored.

The establishment of coal mining in the surrounding area must have caused even more upheaval. In 1856 two shafts were sunk to the High Hazels Seam at 97 yards at Waleswood Colliery, about a mile to the west of the village of Wales and the colliery was deepened *via* two additional shafts to the Barnsley Seam at a depth of 197 yards in 1864. Waleswood Colliery closed in 1948. Kiveton Park Colliery was opened in 1868 less than a mile to the east.

The impact of mining on the village of Wales was immediate and long-lasting. The population of Wales in 1851 before the development of coal mining in the area was 268. By 1901 it had more than trebled to 876. By the latter date male village residents in rural occupations such as farmer, farm foreman, cowman and agricultural labourer were far outnumbered by coal hewers, coal fillers, colliery engine drivers, colliery horsekeepers and pit deputies. The village school, built in 1876, had to be enlarged by 1890 and accommodated 280 children in 1901, more than the entire village population of 1851. And many of the families living in the village in 1901 had no deep local roots. There were many migrants from near and far: from nearby villages and other parts of the West Riding, from neighbouring Derbyshire, Nottinghamshire and Lincolnshire, from Lancashire, Staffordshire, and even Essex and Middlesex. The census enumerator in late March

1901 even delivered a schedule to a tramp living in a stable in the village but by census day on 31 March he had moved to 'Worksop Union'.

Despite its long history as an agricultural village, Wales was rapidly becoming a colliery village just like the relatively newly created one lying to the east of it. And this growth and extension outwards continued during the twentieth century. To the west at Wales Bar, a small outlier of two terraced rows, South Terrace and East Terrace, which survive to this day, had appeared before the First World War and this was followed by a small bungalow estate at the junction of School Road and Mansfield Road. To the east of the old village almost reaching Kiveton Park, the Limetree estate was built in the 1920s to the north of Wales Road and then to the south of the same road in the immediate post-war period the 'White City' was built, an estate of prefabs, now replaced by modern housing.

Three-quarters of a mile to the east of the village of Wales a completely new colliery settlement, Kiveton Park, had emerged since the late 1860s. The colliery and the new village were built on either side of the Great Central Railway (originally the Manchester, Sheffield and Lincolnshire Railway, opened in 1847) immediately to the south-west of the hamlet of Kiveton and the former landscaped park and mansion of the Duke of Leeds. It was Thomas Osborne, later the Duke of Leeds who called his mansion Kiveton Park. The mansion dating from the late eighteenth century was demolished in 1811 and the surrounding park converted back into farmland.

The railway connected the colliery directly with the large industrial market of Sheffield eleven miles to the north west and Grimsby docks on the north Lincolnshire coast, for the export market. The sinking of the colliery started in June 1866, the Barnsley Seam was reached at just over 400 yards in December 1867 and production began in 1868. In the mid-1880s the workings were deepened to the Thorncliffe Seam at 669 yards and to the Silkstone Seam at 733 yards. In the mid-1870s two more shafts were sunk to the Barnsley Seam at West Kiveton Colliery, a mile to the west of Kiveton Park along the Killamarsh Branch of the Midland Railway. The colliery did not close until 1994 when it was still employing 273 men.

Unlike Wales, which had been in existence for at least 900 years, Kiveton Park as a village community, was less that 35 years old at the beginning of the twentieth century. Yet by that time it had outstripped its ancient neighbour and its population stood at more than 1,500. But there was no manor house, no ancient church, and no vicarage in Kiveton Park. And whereas the church, the farmhouses and old cottages in the village of Wales were built of stone, Kiveton Park was built almost entirely of brick. Virtually everyone lived in a cottage in a terraced row. At the western entrance to the village there were two rows, Carrington and Dawson, which still survive, named after the two men responsible for the sinking of Kiveton Park Colliery in 1867. Beyond these, across the railway to the south of Wales Road, lay a collection of seven terraced rows which went under the intimidating title of 'The Barracks' on the 1901 25-inch Ordnance Survey map. Beyond these separated by a large area of allotment gardens were Kiveton Rows. Besides the housing and shops, there was a school which was built in 1874 (before that date school classes were held in the colliery offices), and which in 1901 accommodated 490 children, a Primitive Methodist chapel (erected in 1873) and a workmen's club. When not at work, at chapel or in the workmen's club, many hours would be spent by the miners in tending their allotments, these vegetable and flower gardens covering more than 23 acres.

Apart from shopkeepers (there were grocers, beer retailers, a newsagent, a draper, a butcher, a tailor, a boot dealer, a sub-postmaster and a branch of Worksop Co-operative Society) almost all the other male employed residents in 1901 worked at the colliery in such occupations as coal hewer, filler, pony driver, trammer, ripper, platelayer, checkweighman, deputy, and 'pit corporal'. And like most of their coal mining neighbours in Wales, many of these colliery workers had been born outside the West Riding in counties as far apart as Derbyshire, Nottinghamshire, Leicestershire, Warwickshire, Gloucestershire, Oxfordshire, Northamptonshire, Norfolk and Suffolk. The original sinkers of the colliery in 1866 and 1867 had come from the south Derbyshire mining village of Church Gresley, and in 1901 there were still some miners living and working at Kiveton Park who had been born in Church Gresley and the neighbouring settlements of Swadlincote and Woodville.

Figure 3.8 The Colliery Offices at Kiveton Park.

This purpose-built mining settlement, like Wales to the west, expanded northwards and eastwards in the inter-war and post-war periods, north of Station Road and to Red Hill in the east. Today the two settlements have merged to form one largely suburban community. Two remaining reminders of Kiveton Park's mining past are the pithead baths dating from 1938 and the colliery offices built in 1872, the latter with its tall clock tower with one face built deliberately facing the village (Figure 3.8). The clock in the clock tower still tells the right time. The building has been refurbished and is now a community centre.

Chapter 4

Once Small Villages on the Exposed Coalfield Expanded into Mining Communities through Infilling and Extension

An important feature of the development of housing for the mining population on the exposed coalfield of South Yorkshire was the way in which existing settlements, most, but not all of them, rural villages, expanded to become mining villages. And this happened in different ways. In some villages gaps were filled in the existing layout, in others new additions, some small others very large, were built and in yet others a combination of small-scale infilling and the building of residential 'adjuncts' took place. There are numerous examples of each type. In this chapter a number of villages are examined in which infilling was a major early feature followed only later by peripheral expansion. Dodworth is a clear example of a village where early residential expansion took place through infilling and only later expanded outwards; and in Carlton, Bolton upon Dearne, Thorpe Hesley, and Mapplewell/Staincross, both infilling and peripheral expansion took place over time. Birdwell looks like a very long street village along Sheffield Road but its long sinuous shape resulted from a small core off the main road being infilled and added to. Scholes, a very near neighbour of Thorpe Hesley, is an odd example where there was little physical change in the village and the men and boys already living there merely changed their occupation with households sometimes augmented by lodgers.

Dodworth

Dodworth, on a broad spur between two easterly flowing streams had an important role to play in the local and regional economy many centuries before it became a mining village. It was dry and the spur and the village street that grew up upon it became part of an important land route that went westwards over the Pennines and eastwards in the direction of Doncaster. It was the salt route from Cheshire and eventually became a turnpike road (The Doncaster and Saltersbrook Trust). A house on the southern side of High Street at the western end of the village is still called Salter Croft. Two subsidiary settlements also grew up at some unknown date around two small areas of common, at Dodworth Green and Dodworth Bottom. The main part of the pre-industrial village of Dodworth, on either side of the straight main street between the crossroads in the west and the *Pheasant Inn* in the east has some characteristics of a planned medieval village with the farms of the medieval landlord lying on either side of the wide village street, each farm lying at the street end of a long narrow and straight-sided enclosure called a croft.

This simple settlement pattern underwent considerable internal change in the nineteenth century as a result of railway construction and coal mining development. The Penistone to Barnsley branch of the Manchester, Sheffield and Lincolnshire Railway (from 1897 the Great Central Railway), which crossed Dodworth township less than a quarter of a mile from the village reached Dodworth Station in 1854 and the company's goods station in Barnsley in 1857. This meant that the rich Silkstone Seam was likely to be exploited on a large scale from a new colliery near the new railway. The seam, which was about four and a half feet thick, was of great purity and in great demand as a house and coking coal. The Old Silkstone Colliery (first known as the Church Lane Colliery) was sunk in 1858 to the Silkstone Seam at 205 yards on land acquired from the Brooke family by the Charlesworth brothers, Wakefield colliery proprietors, who sold it in 1862 to the Old Silkstone Coal & Dodworth Iron Company. In 1879 the colliery was closed due to flooding of the Silkstone Seam and it was not re-opened until 1899 by Old Silkstone, Collieries Ltd. This company ran the colliery until nationalisation in 1947. Other seams exploited were Flockton, Parkgate, Thorncliffe and Whinmoor. The colliery eventually closed in June 1987.

The opening of Old Silkstone Colliery and other smaller ones in the vicinity owned by the same company (e.g. Silkstone Fall colliery (sunk in 1871) and Stanhope Silkstone) both to the west) had a marked effect on population growth. In 1801 the population of Dodworth was only 403. By 1851 it had grown to 1,500, the result of coal mining development on the northern and southern borders of the township at Higham and Strafford collieries respectively and domestic handloom linen weaving. This had justified the building of St John's Anglican parish church where the first service was held in February 1846. There was a sharp rise in population in the 1850s and it had reached 2,117 in 1861. By 1901 it had increased to 3,022.

Colliery development near the village of Dodworth did not result in the nineteenth century in the emergence of a distinct new colliery settlement or a large new residential adjunct to the settlement. Instead there was infilling of gaps within the existing settlement. Some infilling had gone on from the early nineteenth century to accommodate linen weavers and their looms but by the beginning of the twentieth century these cottagers were occupied by miners and further miners' cottages were built in the remaining spaces. Silver Street at Dodworth Bottom (which still survives), where 61 miners were living in 1891, is typical of this type of development (Figure 4.1). The cottages in the in-filled Jermyn Croft behind High Street were also the homes of more than 40 miners in 1891. Outward growth at this stage was the exception, the most obvious example being the 30 houses on Station Road between the *Station Inn* and the railway station very near to Old Silkstone Colliery. The pair nearest the station were built in 1901 and called Belmont View (Belmont = beautiful view = of Old Silkstone spoil heap?).

By the beginning of the twentieth century Dodworth had all the other characteristics of a thriving South Yorkshire mining village: a brass band, a working men's club with its mechanics institute, a public house called the *Miners' Inn* (at Dodworth Bottom), a branch of the Yorkshire Penny Bank and a branch (No 2) of the Barnsley British Co-operative Society. And the village

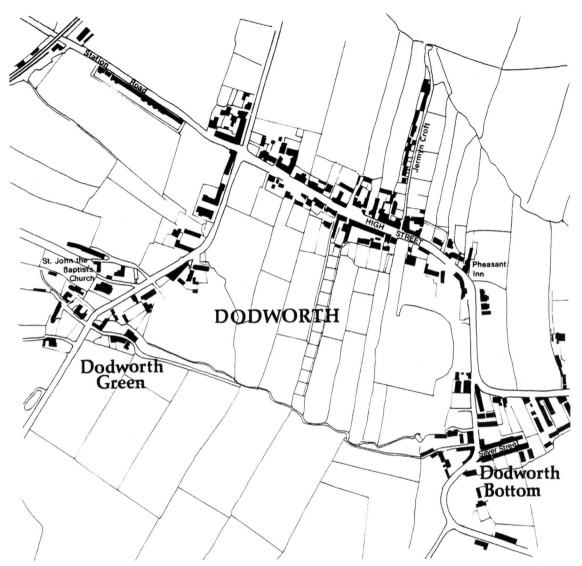

Figure 4.1 Dodworth at the beginning of the twentieth century, based on the 25-inch OS map published in 1906.

was not just populated by miners and their families, shopkeepers, innkeepers and other business people. Living at The Grove, an attractive seventeenth-century house in the High Street was Howard Aston Allport (1842–1915), owner of the Wharncliffe Woodmoor Colliery at Carlton. A previous occupier had been Henry Richardson, one of Barnsley's most important Victorian linen manufacturers.

In the first half of the twentieth century the village expanded westwards in the form of Hawthorne Crescent and eastwards on Gate Crescent and South Road. Since then, it has expanded in almost every direction and now with a population of nearly 5,800 is a popular peripheral suburb of

Barnsley because of its location near junction 37 of the M1 motorway. The site of Old Silkstone Colliery has been landscaped and is now part of the Fall Bank industrial estate and Dodworth Business Park and the spoil heap has been planted up as a mixed woodland, and to newcomers looks like part of the natural landscape.

Carlton

Carlton had two collieries, both of which had eventful histories. In 1870 Joshua Willey from Hoyland leased land from the Earl of Wharncliffe and sank two shafts of what he called Willey New Colliery to the south-west of the village north of Carlton Road down to the Woodmoor Seam at the shallow depth of only 40 yards. Within just a year or two Willey sold the colliery and a new colliery company was formed called the Wharncliffe Woodmoor Coal Company. The company intended to operate from four shafts exploiting in addition to the Woodmoor Seam, the Two Foot Seam and the Winter Seam. The colliery changed hands twice again during the 1880s. From the 1890s coke ovens were in operation and in the twentieth century four more seams were exploited: the Beamshaw, High Hazel, Kent's Thick and Lidgett. For most of its life the colliery was known as Wharncliffe Woodmoor 1, 2 &3 or Old Carlton. It closed in 1966.

While Old Carlton Colliery was in its very early years another colliery was being sunk to the east of the village, almost halfway between Carlton and Cudworth by the Yorkshire & Derbyshire Coal & Iron Company. As in the case Old Carlton the colliery was on land belonging to the Earl of Wharncliffe who cut the first sod on 12 November 1873. Originally it was called Carlton Main Colliery. The colliery was closed between 1910 and 1924, and when it re-opened it was renamed Wharncliffe Woodmoor 4 & 5, but was always known locally as New Carlton. In later years a steep drift mine was made to reach the deepest workings. Altogether five seams were exploited at the colliery. It closed in 1970.

The presence of two collieries on either side of the village had a major impact on its population growth, its attraction to migrants and the way that the layout of the village changed. At the beginning of the Victorian period, Carlton was a rural village with a population of a little over 400 in 1841. Between 1841 and 1871 the population declined so that by 1871 it stood at 380. Things changed with the opening of the two collieries. By 1881 it had risen sharply to 1,085 and by 1901 it stood at nearly 2,300. The Long Row (Carlton Terrace) and Stone Row which were located immediately beside Carlton Main (Wharncliffe Woodmoor 4 & 5 Colliery) more than half a mile from the centre of the old village have already been discussed as a new, small isolated mining colony in Chapter 2. In this chapter we look at what was happening in the rest of the village.

The pre-mining village was in the form of a main thoroughfare (Royston Lane) with two back lanes, Chapel Lane and Spring Lane, winding away to the west behind it before joining to become Carlton Road. From this nucleus during its time as a mining village, Carlton grew, slowly in all directions, the result of both infilling and outward extensions. By about 1930, sixty years after the sinking of Old Carlton Colliery, there were ribbon-like extensions along Carlton Road beside the colliery, being called, not surprisingly, Willey Row; along Shaw Lane in the direction of New Carlton Colliery; and at the junction of Fish Dam Lane and Mill Hill Lane to the south of the village, known locally as 'Sticky Top'. There was also a sizeable adjunct to the north-west of the old village between Crookes Lane and Wood Lane dominated by Grays Road and Briggs Street. Infills included allotment gardens, a village club, a miners' welfare recreation ground, a Methodist chapel and a new parish church with its distinctive saddleback roof built at the expense of the Earl of Whancliffe. The new parish of Carlton had been carved out of the much larger parish of Royston in 1879.

But the most intriguing infills of all were built by a Welshman of very high standing living in the village. This was Evan Parry, a migrant from north Wales and manager of Old Carlton Colliery from 1884 to 1911. The appointment of Evan Parry sparked off an important long-distance migration that gave Carlton a distinctive character. Towards the end of the nineteenth century the village of Carlton had become known locally as 'Little Wales'. Its population included 38 families containing nearly 200 people headed by a Welsh-born man employed in coal mining.

The story of this migration begins in the small industrial community of Mostyn in the parish of Whitford on the Welsh side of the Dee estuary in the summer of 1884. At the time the main source of employment in Mostyn was Mostyn Quay Colliery and the adjoining ironworks. The colliery extended under the estuary for more than half a mile and on 19 July 1884 water from the estuary broke into the mine and flooded the workings. The *Flintshire Observer* reported on 24 July 1884 that the 'disastrous occurrence' was 'of the most serious nature for the whole district, as no less than two hundred men and boys have been thrown out of employment'. On 31 July 1884, the same newspaper, under the headline 'The Calamity at Mostyn Colliery' reported that despite continuous pumping since the flooding, the water level in the pit had not yet fallen. It soon became apparent that it was unlikely ever to be operational again. And that indeed was to be the case.

The impact on the community was devastating. Whole families were suddenly without a regular wage and shopkeepers and other businessmen soon began to feel the effect of mass unemployment and then population decline set in as people began to leave the district to seek work elsewhere. Heads of families began to move, often leaving their families in Mostyn and returning at weekends or once a month. When it became increasingly clear that there was little or no hope of Mostyn Quay Colliery ever operating again, the women, with their children, left to join their husbands and older sons in the places where they had found regular colliery work.

Although some of the migrants to England and beyond settled in places as diverse as Manchester, Liverpool and Melton Mowbray in England, and Patagonia, Buenos Aires and Alabama in the Americas, most miners and their families went to a restricted number of places, particularly in south Lancashire, and remained in coal mining. It has been reported that some of the miners took their pit ponies with them to Lancashire, but the ponies would only obey orders given in Welsh!

Figure 4.2 Evan Parry and his wife Anne, founders of the Welsh colony in Carlton and Smithies.

Some of the migrants made their way to the villages of Carlton and Smithies. The connection between Mostyn and South Yorkshire was, of course, Evan Parry. Parry, a native of Mostyn was appointed manager of Wharncliffe Woodmoor 1,2 and 3 ('Old Carlton') Colliery at Carlton in 1884 (Figure 4.2). Without his appointment the Welsh colony would not have come into existence and without his continued guidance, encouragement and commitment it would not have evolved as it did.

Besides Parry's immediate family, other close relatives were important members of the emerging Welsh colony. Both his younger sisters followed their elder brother to Carlton - Anne and her husband Evan Williams and their four children arrived sometime between 1885–91; Catherine and her husband David Davies had also arrived by 1890. Both of Evan Parry's younger brothers also followed him to South Yorkshire. The youngest brother, Enoch, and his family seem to have arrived in the district in about 1888. Evan's other brother, David, who was unmarried in 1891, was lodging with his sister Anne at the time of the census in that year.

Other pioneering families from the Mostyn area living in Carlton by 1891 were those headed by Richard and Elizabeth Jones, Thomas and Sarah Hodgson, Edward and Elizabeth Macdonald and Thomas and Sarah Edwards. In the neighbouring village of Smithies, where David Davies, Enoch Parry and Evan Williams and their families lived, other pioneering families were those headed by Owen and Ann Jones, John and Isabella Jones and John Gittins, a widower in 1891.

Besides these families there were also thirteen lodgers from the Mostyn area listed in the 1891 census. One of these lodgers, David Parry, has already been mentioned. Three others are worthy of notice. David Jones Williams, then in his mid-twenties, was commercial manager at Wharncliffe Woodmoor Colliery where Evan Parry was manager. He was later to rise up and become secretary of the colliery company and then a director. Ithel Macdonald and Thomas Cunnah were both young men (19 and 21 respectively). They were to be major driving forces in the building of the Welsh Chapel at Carlton.

At the time of the 1891 and 1901 censuses, the Welsh colonists were dispersed widely in Carlton and the neighbouring village of Smithies, a reflection of the need for migrants from north Wales to rent housing or take lodgings wherever they happened to be available. There was even one family that had originated in Mostyn living in Westgate in Monk Bretton in 1901. This family headed by John Williams, shows the pull that guaranteed work and life among your own kind had on former miners at Mostyn Quay Colliery, causing a very round-about migration. It is known that John Williams went first to Hanley in Staffordshire where he married. The 1901 census shows that his youngest three children were all born in Carlton, but his three oldest children, all boys, were born in Argentina!

The early 1890s witnessed developments that were to create a physical and cultural focus for the Welsh community in Carlton. Again Evan Parry, the colliery manager, was a prime mover. In 1891 he purchased a partly built house, Brookfield House, on Chapel Lane at Carlton, together with two parcels of land on either side of the lane. By 1901 he had converted Brookfield House into three separate dwellings and built 22 new houses including what are known today as Greenfield Cottages, Southfield Cottages, Gordon Villas, Providence View and Brookfield Terrace (Figure 4.3). By the time of the 1911 census there were 25 families, 124 people in all, living in this small residential enclave. All but one of the 25 heads of household was in an occupation connected with Old Carlton Colliery. The exception was a police constable. The inhabitants included Evan Parry, by that time retired, his wife, three sons (two of whom were hewers and the eldest a certified colliery manager) and seven other families with a Welsh-born head of household. In one of these families, although the husband and wife, Thomas and Esther Jones, had both been born in Flintshire, three of their four children had been born in Golborne in Lancashire, one of the known Lancashire destinations of the migrant miners from Mostyn Colliery. So the Joneses had taken part in a stepwise migration (see Chapter 1). A resident in Brookfield Cottages had been born in Staffordshire, but his wife was from Flintshire as were his two sons, suggesting that he had perhaps migrated from the West Midlands to Wales and then back again to England following the Mostyn Colliery disaster.

Figure 4.3 Providence View (left) and Brookfield Terrace (right), Carlton, two of the seven groups of cottages built at Evan Parry's expense.

As these developments, catering for the physical comforts of the rapidly growing mining community, including members of Evan Parry's family and other key colliery employees were taking place, moves were also afoot to provide for the spiritual needs of the Welsh population. In 1890 it was decided to create a church where, as their pastor was to describe it a few years later, they could 'worship the God of their fathers in their native tongue'. A Welsh church, in the sense of a group of people sharing the same beliefs and worshipping together, was founded in the summer of 1890. The congregation continued to meet in people's homes or rented rooms for the rest of the decade.

At the beginning of 1901, the Reverend Menai Francis, pastor of the church, called a meeting of the senior members of the church to look into the possibility of building a chapel at Carlton. In May 1901, the Earl of Wharncliffe's agent, together with Evan Parry, met the Building Fund Committee at Carlton with a view to selecting a possible site. This was fixed in Carlton Lane adjacent to the land Evan Parry had bought about ten years earlier and on which he had been busy building houses. Subsequently a lease of thirty years was agreed at a rent of 5/- a year. The contract for building the chapel was put in the hands of Walkers of Sheffield who specialised in building corrugated iron buildings including chapels. The chapel was opened on 6 June 1902 (Figure 4.4). It had cost £200 to build.

Figure 4.4 (a) The Welsh chapel at Carlton shortly before its demolition in 1984 and (b) inset, a close-up of the chapel sign in Welsh.

Money to build, furnish and maintain the chapel came from many sources. There were generous donations from members and friends and from the profits from musical concerts. There had been a church choir since 1895 and concerts were given in the Public Hall in Barnsley. It was also the custom from the early days for the choir at Christmas to go round Carlton and to some of the big houses in Barnsley, ending up at *Rhydwen*, the house of David Jones Williams. After performing carols and Welsh hymns they were given refreshments by the Williams family.

The period between the opening of the Chapel in 1902 and the beginning of the First World War in 1914 was the high point in the life of the community. By that time the Anglo-Welsh community must have been several hundred strong (estimates vary from 200–400). Even if individuals or families were not chapel-goers, they had the opportunity to attend the regular events that took place that reminded them of their origins and reinforced their cultural identity. In this period there was still a trickle of in-migrants from North Wales, children of the original migrants had grown up, married and had young families, and many first and second generation members had a strong allegiance to the chapel. The Welsh language was still used in the home as well as at chapel, and occasions such as carol singing around the village at Christmas time,

Whitsuntide outings, musical concerts in Barnsley, and the annual singing festival (*gymanfa ganu*) with other West Riding Welsh chapels (Sheffield, Leeds and later Doncaster) and Welsh societies, had become regular events.

Although marriages took place between members of the Welsh community or between members of the Welsh community and partners from Wales, marriages also occurred between members of the original migrant community and partners from local families or from families who had migrated to Carlton at much the same time as the Welsh community was being formed there. One of Evan Parry's sons married a girl from north Wales but the others chose marriage partners from South Yorkshire of English stock.

The contribution made by Evan Parry in sustaining the community in its early years cannot be overestimated. He provided employment and housing (although his cottages were by no means exclusively occupied by Welsh families) and he arranged a temporary home for the church congregation on Sundays between 1894 and 1902. As manager of Old Carlton Pit, he rearranged shifts so that the church choir could give concerts and no doubt helped in many other ways.

After the First World War, the attrition of the community identity went on relentlessly through marrying out. In some families this happened in one generation. Despite the fact that assimilation was taking place at a rapid rate, the Welsh Chapel continued to prosper in the inter-war period and during the Second World War, fortified periodically by migrants from Wales to the Barnsley district. The annual *Gymanfa* continued till the early 1980s, but by that time chapel membership was less than 20 with no more than a dozen regular attenders, services were held only intermittently, and the building was badly in need of repairs. Reluctantly, the decision was made to close the Chapel permanently. The final service was held in December 1983, with a congregation of over 60. The building was demolished in 1984. There must be hundreds of people still living in the Barnsley area descended from these Welsh in-migrants. Gwen Bright, for example, mayor of Barnsley in 1978–79, was the grand-daughter of Evan Parry's sister.

Bolton upon Dearne

The village of Bolton upon Dearne lies in a striking location in the Dearne valley. The once-rural village stands on a low, shelving diamond-shaped promontory of shale and sandstone (Mexborough Rock) between about 60 and 150 feet (18 and 46 metres) above sea level surrounded on almost all four sides by the alluvial flatlands of the flood plain of the River Dearne. The promontory is about two miles (three kilometres) wide from east to west and one mile (1.6 kilometres) long from north to south. The fact that the slightly elevated land almost reached the River Dearne in the south made the site of the village an important early bridging point. The area covered by the surrounding flood plain can be largely identified by names alone. High Street, for example, on leaving the village to the west becomes Ings Lane, 'ings' being derived from the Old Norse word *eng* meaning a water meadow. To the north, Back Lane on leaving the village to the west eventually becomes Carr Head Lane, *kjarr* being another Old Norse word meaning a marsh covered in woodland, usually of willow and alder. To the south of the village beside the River Dearne is an extensive area called The Holmes and this name is also from an Old Norse word *holmr* meaning an island in a marsh. Lastly a large area to the south of the village is marked on early Ordnance Survey maps as 'Liable to Floods'. Across the other side of the Dearne valley, lies Adwick upon Dearne, occupying a site similar to that of Bolton upon Dearne.

At the beginning of the twentieth century Bolton upon Dearne was not the sprawling settlement of today spreading northwards without a break to Goldthorpe and then with only a small break in the built-up area into Thurnscoe. Quite the opposite was the case. It was small and compact. Although roughly rectangular in shape, such villages are sometimes called 'square villages' or more technically as 'irregular nucleated villages'. The irregular but compact shape of such a village as this is usually attributed to its gradual expansion over a long period of time from an isolated farm or hamlet into a village through the practice of divided land inheritance and the subsequent multiplication of family and farm units. The fact that Bolton upon Dearne started out as a single homestead is reflected in its name. It appeared in writing for the first time in the Domesday Book in 1086 as Bodeltone, an Anglo-Saxon (Old English) name *bodel* meaning buildings and *tun* meaning a farmstead, and later a village. The fact that the buildings were singled out for mention in its name suggests that it was more than a simple farmstead, perhaps a substantial manor house.

The village seems to have developed on both sides of an east-west running street, High Street, probably from an original nucleus at the eastern end where the parish church, the Manor Farm and *The Angel* public house all stood. To the north of High Street, and running parallel to it is Back Lane, a feature found in many English villages. To the south of the churchyard is New Street, a misleading name for a thoroughfare that could be many centuries old.

The most imposing building in the village at the beginning of the twentieth century set on a slight knoll, with its tall sixteenth-century tower, was still the parish church, dedicated to St Andrew. Its Anglo-Saxon foundation is confirmed by traces of Anglo-Saxon masonry in the lower part of the exterior walls of the nave (which was the original Anglo-Saxon church), massive long-and-short quoins at the corners of the nave and an Anglo-Saxon slit window. Another ancient feature in the village at the beginning of the twentieth century was the old pinfold near the corner of Church Street and Angel Street. Outside the village, to the south on the River Dearne were two corn mills, each with a mill race that once turned the water wheels that powered them.

At first glance, at the beginning of the twentieth century, Bolton upon Dearne looks from cartographic evidence like a typical English rural village located deep in the countryside completely unaffected by the rapid industrialization that was taking place throughout South Yorkshire. Nothing could be further from the truth. Just two miles to the north in Thurnscoe was Hickleton Main Colliery. Shafts began to be sunk there in 1892 and by 1895 the colliery was producing half a million tons of coal and in 1898 employed 900 men and boys underground and 200 on the surface. About a mile to the south and south-east were two more collieries: Manvers

Main and Wath Main. Manvers Main consisted of two collieries 650 yards apart, the first coal being raised in 1870. The first coal from Wath Main was raised in 1879.

There were also two railways running through the countryside near the village, one carried passengers and freight but the other was built to carry coal. This was the Wath branch of the Hull and Barnsley railway. The main line of this railway, from Stairfoot near Barnsley to Alexandra Dock in Hull, was opened in 1885, but the Wath branch was not opened until 31 March 1902. The railway gave direct access to Hull and overseas markets for coal from Wath Main, Manvers Main and Hickleton Main.

It is not surprising, then, that the 1901 census recorded not only farmers, farmworkers and village tradesmen such as joiners, millers and wheelwrights in Bolton upon Dearne but also those engaged in the coal mining industry and working on the railways. It has already been noted that one railway running near the village in 1901 had been opened just over twenty years earlier and that another was under construction. No wonder then that among the village inhabitants were men and boys employed in a host of railway occupations from a station master, railway shunters and engine drivers to railway platelayers, railway labourers and railway navvies. The majority of men and boys however – householders, their sons and boarders – worked in neighbouring collieries in 1901. And at this time most of these railway workers and coal miners lived within the confines of the original rural village or in very small extensions to it.

As a result of the expansion of railway employment and particularly the rapid eastward development of the South Yorkshire coalfield in the second half of the nineteenth century the population of Bolton upon Dearne, like that in all the surrounding settlements, had grown at a tremendous rate. In 1851 the population of the parish (i.e. including Goldthorpe) was 604. By 1881 it had risen to just over 1,000, by 1891 to 1,205 and by 1901 to 3,827. The growth was due not only to the rapid birth rate but principally to the very high level of in-migration. In 1901, although there were short distance migrants from neighbouring villages, there were living in Bolton upon Dearne in-migrants from virtually every part of the British Isles. Take Lady Croft, for example, comprising two facing rows of 50 terraced houses between High Street and Back Lane, that formed an important early residential 'infill' in the village (Figure 4.5). Only fourteen heads of household living there in 1901 were born in Bolton upon Dearne. There were in-migrant heads of household and boarders from other parts of South Yorkshire including, for example, from Barnburgh, Barnsley, Bentley, Kimberworth, Wath and Wombwell. They had also arrived from West Yorkshire: from Batley, Honley and Kirkburton. There were also those from the neighbouring counties of Derbyshire, Lincolnshire and Nottinghamshire and from the more distant counties of Staffordshire, Warwickshire and Worcestershire. They had also arrived from the southern counties of Essex, Gloucestershire and Somerset and there were even a couple of Londoners and some from Ireland. And some of these in-migrants had come from very small places deep in the English countryside: Steeple Aston in Oxfordshire and Green Bottom in Gloucestershire. Green Bottom is still a tiny tucked-way hamlet in the Forest of Dean.

Figure 4.5 Bolton upon Dearne as shown on the 25-inch OS map published in 1904.

But it was not only the manual workers in the coal industry who made their homes in Bolton upon Dearne. Living at Bolton Hall until his untimely death at the early age of 55 in 1895 was Joseph Mitchell, an important local coal owner and a member of what has been called the 'new aristocracy' of men who had made names for themselves not from descent through noble families but from their careers in industry and business. Joseph Mitchell lived in luxury compared to the railway workers and coal miners who lived only a very short distance away. Their small houses were absolutely crammed with residents, up to a dozen people, the parents and either their children or boarders or a combination of both. But at Bolton Hall the house and its outbuildings covered roughly the same area as 50 houses in Lady Croft in the middle of the village. And although there were fourteen people living at the hall, seven of these were family members, one was a visitor and six were servants: a cook, a kitchen maid, two housemaids, a sundry maid and a nurse.

Joseph Mitchell was the son of Joseph Mitchell who had founded the Worsbrough Dale Foundry that supplied steam engines and boilers to local collieries, bridges for the local railway system and coal wagons. In 1852 Joseph Mitchell senior had sunk Edmunds Main Colliery at Worsbrough Dale and later Swaithe Main colliery in the same place. In 1871 Joseph Mitchell senior began to sink Mitchell Main Colliery to the north of Wombwell but he died in 1875 when work was still underway. The company also acquired Darfield Main Colliery. On 8 October 1894 Joseph Mitchell junior, less than a year before his death, as managing director of the Mitchell Main Colliery Company, presided over a 'Turning of the First Sod' ceremony at Grimethorpe Colliery. Between 1890 and 1892 he was president of the Midland Institute of Mining, Civil and Mechanical Engineers and in 1892 was appointed Justice of the Peace. He was a churchwarden of St Andrew's church at Bolton upon Dearne and gave the pews in the nave in 1890 to replace the old oak box pews. The font in the church was presented in his memory by the congregation and his friends. Bolton Hall was largely demolished in 1970.

Bolton upon Dearne expanded outwards, mostly to the north, during the twentieth century and now forms one continuous built-up area stretching to Goldthorpe and Thurnscoe, a distance of three miles (3.1 kilometers).

Thorpe Hesley and Scholes

Thorpe Hesley and its much smaller neighbour Scholes have had a very long and complicated association with mines and mining. Opposite the top of Scholes Lane on what used to be called Thorpe Common is a group of restored stone buildings that were named Kirkstead Abbey Grange by their owner the Earl of Effingham in 1900, after they had lain empty for more than forty years. Before that they had formerly been houses and barns of Parkgate Farm but were known informally as the Monks' Smithy Houses. This was because the main group of buildings, in the form of a laithehouse or longhouse, were believed to be the much altered and re-built remains of the headquarters of a monastic grange, i.e. an outlying economic unit belonging to a monastic house. This grange was concerned with the mining of ironstone and the making of iron. In 1161 the monks of Kirkstead Abbey in Lincolnshire were granted land by the lord of the manor of Kimberworth, Richard de Builli, on which to mine ironstone and to have two furnaces and two forges to make iron. This is the first documented record of metal working in the Sheffield and Rotherham areas. They were also granted 200 acres in the adjoining Ecclesfield parish by the lord of the manor of Hallamshire, Richard de Lovetot. This monastic economic activity went on for at least a century. No wonder then that the area today, including the remains of Thorpe Common, agricultural land and local woods, is still peppered with ironstone bell pit mounds, some of them no doubt of medieval origin.

Although nailmaking had always been an important 'cottage' industry in Thorpe and Scholes, and although at that time there were no collieries in the village, a surprising number of local men and boys were employed in mining at the time of the 1841 census. At that time the population of Thorpe Hesley was 1,239 and Scholes had a population of 315. Of the 446 males living in Thorpe Hesley for whom occupations were given, 82 (18 per cent) were engaged in farming, 130 (29 per cent) in nailmaking and 202 (45 per cent) in mining. Of the 78 males living in Scholes for whom occupations were given in 1841, 17 (22 per cent) were in farming, 11 (14 per cent) were nailmakers and 31 (40 per cent) were miners. And in some Thorpe families in 1841 there were both ironstone and coal miners. Some of the ironstone miners at that time worked in the ironstone pits in Tankersley Park that supplied Milton and Elsecar Ironworks in Hoyland. In 1850 ironstone mining records in the Wentworth Woodhouse Muniments reveal that 22 of the 250 men and boys mining ironstone in the park were from Thorpe and travelled four miles on a round trip there and back every working day. Coal and ironstone miners from Thorpe and Scholes must also have been working in the pits belonging to Newton Chambers in the area between Thorpe Hesley, Chapeltown and High Green.

Ironstone mining was no longer taking place after 1880 but small collieries were dotted about the area. In 1881 in Scholes out of an adult male population of 102, no fewer than 88 were coalminers. The 1901 25-inch Ordnance Survey map shows Scholes Old Colliery on Little Lane halfway between Scholes and Thorpe, where two small slag heaps still survive, and Scholes Colliery behind Upper Wortley Road on Thorpe Common. These two collieries belonged to the Mangham family. It is also worthy of note that Arthur Mangham, the owner of Scholes Colliery, and his son Bertrand, played a leading part, for a decade before the First World War in opening up the coal mining industry in Spitzbergen in the Arctic Circle.

The further expansion of Thorpe Hesley as a mining community dates from the sinking of four collieries by Newton Chambers that were linked to each other in various ways. These were Norfolk Colliery, Smithy Wood Colliery, Barley Hall Colliery and Thorpe Colliery. The Silkstone Seam was reached at Barley Hall Colliery half a mile to the west of Thorpe Hesley in 1887 and eventually six seams were worked there. Thorpe Pit was sunk on the edge of the village between 1900 and 1903. Barley Hall and Thorpe collieries were exceptional in that they were not connected to a railway and coal was never wound to the surface there. They were ventilation shafts, service shafts and water pumping shafts for Norfolk, Smithy Wood (sunk in 1890) and Thorncliffe (sunk in 1859) collieries. Thorpe Colliery closed in 1972, Smithy Wood closed in the same year and Barley Hall in 1975. Shortly after its closure the site of Thorpe Colliery had a most unusual function on two occasions. In 1975, when the buildings and winding gear were still in place, it was used to film scenes for the Disney feature film *Escape from the Dark* (in the USA re-titled *The Littlest Horse Thieves*) starring Alastair Sim and Peter Barkworth. It told the story of three children trying to save three pit ponies from the slaughterhouse after the pit had been mechanized. The following year it was used by the BBC to film the outdoor scenes on the BBC adaptation of Barry Hines' *The Price of Coal*. In both films local people worked as extras.

The impact of mining on the size and shape of Thorpe Hesley was patchy (Figure 4.6). Between 1850 and the beginning of the twentieth century, there was some infilling and extension at the bottom of Brook Hill and on Hesley Lane in the existing village and a short row of cottages was built at right angles to Barnsley Road next to Barley Hall Colliery. And between the two world wars, on the south side of Barnsley Road just north of its junction with Thorpe Street opposite Kirby Row, Newton Chambers built a small estate of semi-detached houses for senior

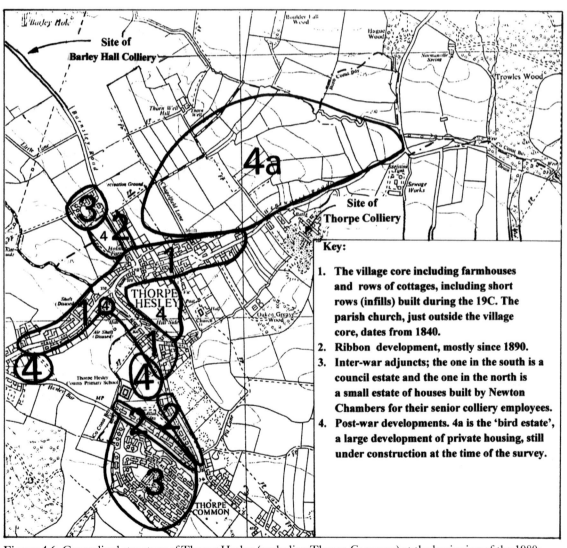

Key:

1. The village core including farmhouses and rows of cottages, including short rows (infills) built during the 19C. The parish church, just outside the village core, dates from 1840.
2. Ribbon development, mostly since 1890.
3. Inter-war adjuncts; the one in the south is a council estate and the one in the north is a small estate of houses built by Newton Chambers for their senior colliery employees.
4. Post-war developments. 4a is the 'bird estate', a large development of private housing, still under construction at the time of the survey.

Figure 4.6 Generalised structure of Thorpe Hesley (excluding Thorpe Common) at the beginning of the 1980s.

colliery officials. These reverted to the National Coal Board on nationalisation and survive to this day. Little changed to the physical fabric in the neighbouring village of Scholes. Over time in Scholes it was simply a matter of changing jobs from farm labourer, estate worker at Wentworth Woodhouse and nailmaker to miner.

Thorpe Hesley today is barely recognisable as a former mining village. The site of Thorpe Colliery is now covered with scrub woodland as is the site of Barley Hall Colliery which was landscaped and the short row of terraced cottages was buried beneath the landscaped site. In the last 30–40 years there has been much infilling with new brick-built houses and apartments and a major residential adjunct, the 'bird estate', where every street name is the name of a bird. The village is now a dormitory settlement conveniently located next to junction 35 on the M1 motorway. And as for Scholes, there has been some new housing built around Scholes Green and renovation and new building on the long winding village street, but basically its shape and size has altered little over the centuries. But now it has been gentrified to an extent that some locals refer to it as 'Millionaire's Row'. This characterization is very different from the damning description of Scholes by John Thomas in his *Walks in the Neighbourhood of Sheffield* in 1844:

Houses – not cottages – and these of most Irish aspect, salute the traveller, and bid him remember how closely tacked to the silken skirts of aristocracy is the frieze and worsted of helot labour and poverty. The entrance to Scholes is positively displeasing: if the tastes and habits of the miners dwelling therein, demand and require no better accommodation, being the free tenants of an earl, and breathing the air common to his princely palace, occasion might be taken to give them the liking and use of better habitations.

Birdwell

Today a visitor passing through the area is under the impression that Birdwell is simply a very narrow street village stretching along the Sheffield Road (A6135) for more than half a mile, from Balk Farm in the north to the tangle of roundabouts in the south at junction 36 of the M1 and the beginning of the Dearne Valley Parkway (Figure 4.7).

It is said that the place got its name from the fact that locals noticed that birds drank from a spring, and so they assumed that the water was uncontaminated and it became the source of their drinking water. Two wells are marked at Birdwell on the first Six-Inch Ordnance Survey map published in 1855, one of them, at the junction of Pilley Lane and Rockley Lane being named simply Bird Well.

In the middle of the nineteenth century Birdwell was no more than a hamlet, not on the main Sheffield Road (which was at this time a turnpike road), but off the main road to the west clustered around the crossroads where Rockley Lane met Pilley Lane and the modern Chapel Street. At the eastern end of Chapel Street was a new development called New End containing two terraced

Figure 4.7 Sheffield Road, Birdwell in 2016.

rows, Robinson Row and Parker Row. Between New End and Birdwell proper was a Wesleyan Methodist chapel. *The Cock* public house was already there at the western edge of the hamlet and on the turnpike road stood the *Old Travellers' Inn*.

Small as it was, Birdwell was already an important local mining settlement. In 1851 there were 178 employed men and boys living there and of these 89 (50 per cent) were miners. Of these, 47 were coal miners and 42 were ironstone miners. It is assumed that the coal miners must have walked to Elsecar or Worsbrough Dale to their work but we know that in 1849 all the ironstone miners were working in the ironstone pits in Tankersley Park that supplied the Milton and Elsecar Ironworks in Hoyland. In 1849 there were 100 men and boys employed at the Tankersley ironstone grounds with 12 teams working in small bell pits and two teams in a deep pit. The records give name, place of residence and for those under 20 years of age, their ages. Based on age it is possible to suggest what job each miner did. For example, John Edgar's team from Birdwell consisted of eight men and boys as follows:

John Edgar	Birdwell	
Benj Hawkins	Tankersley	
Geo Noble	Birdwell	
Saml Mitchell	Tankersley	
Like Noble	Birdwell	15
Edw Sylvester	Birdwell	16
Chas Sylvester	Birdwell	10
Wm Ward	Birdwell	10

Of the four adults, the two oldest would have worked as a hanger-on (attaching the corves (wagons) full of ironstone to the ropes and chains ready to be wound up the shaft) or as a banksman (who emptied the corves and tipped the ironstone onto a bank), the ones still in their prime would be the getters, working with pick and shovel to get the ironstone, the older teenagers would be trammers, taking the ironstone in the corves to the pit bottom and the youngest would have been gin boys, operating a pulley system by leading a horse or pony round a circle at the pit top.

By the beginning of the twentieth century the ironstone was no longer exploited but collieries had sprung up. In the immediate neighbourhood: Wharncliffe Silkstone Colliery and Rockingham Colliery just to the south in 1854 and 1875 respectively; Hoyland Silkstone just to the east in 1876 and Barrow Colliery about a mile to the north-east also in 1876. The ironstone miners, their descendants and newcomers became in the main coal miners. This is confirmed by analysis of the 1901 census. In 1901 there were 247 employed men and boys living in Birdwell. Of these 199 (81 per cent) were coal miners, ranging from pit deputies and colliery engine winding men to trammers and pit pony drivers. Ten individuals (four per cent) worked in local foundries and the rest covered a wide range of occupations including innkeepers, shopkeepers, a farm bailiff, a barm (yeast) carter and even a professional footballer!

Although outsiders had been attracted to the growing village it is surprising how many of the employed male population were native to the village or were relatively short-distance migrants. Forty-eight (nearly 19 per cent) had been born in Birdwell itself and a further 72 were from elsewhere in Worsbrough township, so that altogether 48 per cent were very locally born. A further 90 individuals were from the rest of Yorkshire including neighbouring villages such as Hoyland, Wentworth and Tankersley and more distant places like Huddersfield, Leeds and Bradford. There were also migrants from 15 other counties, and one each from Scotland, Ireland and Wales. There was even one man who had been born in Nova Scotia, Canada. Some individuals had been born in tiny villages hundreds of miles away from Birdwell, for instance Witchampton in Dorset and Yaxley in Suffolk.

Now the site of the nearest colliery, Rockingham Colliery that closed in 1975 is a business park with an Aldi superstore on the southern edge beside the A6135 and opposite across the road the old Mines Rescue Station dating from 1902 is now occupied by a hairdresser and a beauty parlour!

Mapplewell and Staincross

The former hamlets of Mapplewell and Staincross are just to the east of Darton in the Dearne valley north-west of Barnsley. They all lie in what was originally the ecclesiastical parish of Darton. The conversion of the agricultural village of Darton and its two neighbouring smaller settlements into mining communities is particularly interesting because it was not a matter of three small agriculturally-based settlements being transformed through the sinking of a colliery. The two smaller communities continued for many years to have a quite different important source of employment besides coal mining.

Before the sinking of a deep colliery, small-scale coal mining did take place there because no fewer than eight coal seams outcrop in this part of the Dearne valley. And the small collieries continued to operate even after the deep colliery was sunk. It was the coming of the Lancashire and Yorkshire Railway in 1850 from Barnsley to Horbury along the Dearne valley, less than a mile from Staincross and Mapplewell and near the edge of Darton, that led to the Thorp family of Gawber Hall financing the sinking of North Gawber Colliery between 1850 and 1852, just to the south of the existing village of Mapplewell. Gawber Hall lay to the south across the River Dearne, hence the name of the new colliery, North Gawber. The colliery was linked to the railway by a short mineral line. The thick and valuable Barnsley Seam was reached at a depth of just over 100 yards. It is said that this led to 'great rejoicing in the parish' with the church bells being rung at Darton (Dearnley, n.d.). In later years six other seams were exploited. In 1882 the colliery was acquired by Fountain & Burnley who were also to become the owners of the nearby Woolley Colliery, located not in Woolley village but in the open countryside to the north of Darton. They continued to own both collieries until nationalisation. In the early 1890s coke ovens were also constructed at North Gawber and by the end of the century the colliery employed more than 600 men and boys. Shortly after nationalisation (in 1948), North Gawber took over the smaller and short-lived Darton Hall Colliery (opened in 1914) but in 1986 North Gawber itself was merged with Woolley Colliery. In 1988 both collieries were closed.

Before the sinking of North Gawber Colliery the main source of income in Mapplewell and Staincross was nailmaking which was largely a 'cottage' industry with the craftsmen working in small workshops near to or attached to their cottages. Detailed research by Harold Taylor (Taylor, 1994) has revealed that in 1841, just a decade before the sinking of North Gawber Colliery, of the 282 heads of household living in Mapplewell and Staincross 138 (49 per cent) were engaged in nailmaking. There were only 37 (13 percent) working in farming and only 28 (a mere 10 per cent) were coal miners.

In the second half of the nineteenth century hand nailmaking declined rapidly as machine-made nails cornered the market, and the nailmaking population shrank and aged, and migrants flooded into the two settlements to work in the collieries. This can be illustrated by an analysis of the Carr Green area of Mapplewell (just to the south of North Gawber Colliery) in 1901. In that year the population of Carr Green totalled 172, living in 29 separate households. Household size varied between one (a widow living on her own) and 10. Nine households contained boarders as well as family members. The population included 53 employed men and boys of whom 51 were employed at the colliery. Of these 53 employed men and boys, four had been born in neighbouring Darton, and four in Staincross. None had been born in Mapplewell. And as usual the birthplaces of the 45 employed migrants covered a very wide area. Some had originated from not very far away, for example Barnsley, Ardsley and Worsbrough Dale; others were from West Yorkshire (e.g., Bradford, Dewsbury and Batley) and neighbouring counties (e.g., Liverpool and Wigan in Lancashire, Clowne and Walton in Derbyshire and Retford in Nottinghamshire). There were also four migrants who had been born in Staffordshire. There were, as usual, migrants who had been born in tiny villages in distant, mainly rural, counties, for example a hewer from Runton in Norfolk, a colliery wagon shunter from Marston in Bedfordshire and a colliery labourer from Aldringham in Suffolk There was also one migrant, a hewer at the colliery, who had been born in County Leitrim in western Ireland.

The impact of population growth related to the expansion of deep mining on the settlements was immediate and long lasting. Darton eventually merged with the hamlet of Kexbrough to the west along Church Field Lane and with Mapplewell and Staincross to the east via Bloomhouse Lane to Darton Lane Head and along Darton Lane. Mapplewell and Staincross grew outwards and merged into each other. As in most other villages on the exposed coalfield, much late nineteenth century development was in the form of rows of terraced houses (Figure 4.8). The settlement at Woolley Colliery remained separated from Darton and Staincross by woods and farmland (see

Figure 4.8 Pye Avenue, Mapplewell. (*Old Barnsley*)

Chapter 2). In 1801 the combined population of Kexbrough, Darton, Mapplewell and Staincross was 1,609 and by 1851, when North Gawber Colliery was being sunk, it had risen to 5,565. By the end of the century it had grown to more than 7,600 and it continued to grow in the first half of the twentieth century reaching 14,400 by 1951.

George Orwell in his *Road to Wigan Pier* (1937), his searing and no holds barred account of poverty in the industrial districts of Lancashire and Yorkshire, described a miner's cottage in Mapplewell at the time. It was a 'two up, one down' cottage rented from a private landlord for five shillings a week. The sink was in the living room. There was dry rot in the upstairs floors and 'bugs' infested the house that were kept in check with sheep dip. The road past the house was not asphalted and was said to be almost impassable in winter. The stone lavatories at the end of the gardens were in a ruinous condition. Orwell ranted on about the housing conditions and the housing shortage in industrial districts throughout the country. He obviously never visited the newer mining settlements in the eastern part of the exposed coalfield and on the concealed coalfield, designed and constructed on behalf of the mining companies (see Chapters 6 and 7). Nor did he describe the new council estates of semi-detached houses with their own indoor bathrooms and toilets that were starting to spring up on the edges of mining villages across South Yorkshire, including Mapplewell and Staincross.

Now the northern part of the site once occupied by North Gawber Colliery and its pit heaps is occupied by a Co-operative superstore and industrial units, and at the time of writing the southern half of the site was in the early stages of a large private housing development.

Chapter 5

Once Small Villages on the Exposed Coalfield Expanded into Mining Communities mainly through Peripheral Expansion

In the last chapter, village expansion through infilling and peripheral growth was discussed. This chapter deals with those mining villages where growth was concentrated in peripheral extensions to the settlements. Pilley, Kilnhurst, High Green, Treeton, Darfield, Royston, Thurnscoe, Goldthorpe, Wath upon Dearne, Cudworth and Dinnington are all clear examples of where a once rural hamlet or small village expanded into a mining village mainly through the construction of peripheral areas of new housing. In some cases this was gradual, almost street by street, but in others a large new adjunct was built onto the existing village.

Pilley

This small ancient hamlet in the parish of Tankersley that was first mentioned in the Domesday book of 1086, and whose name means 'the woodland clearing from which wooden shafts were obtained', was completely transformed after the opening of Wharncliffe Silkstone Colliery in 1854. But before that time, things had not altogether stood still in the village. From the end of the eighteenth century men and boys had been employed in local ironstone pits in Tankersley Park just a short distance to the south-east which belonged to Earl Fitzwilliam of Wentworth Woodhouse, and to the north of the village on land owned by the Vernon Wentworths of Wentworth Castle at Stainborough. This was followed by the opening of a small colliery, Pilley Hills Colliery, which was connected by a mineral railway in the early 1830s to the Dearne and Dove Canal at Worsbrough basin. This mineral line was also connected to the ironstone pits to the north of the village. In 1851 there were 111 working men and boys living in Pilley of whom 23 (20.7 per cent) were working in agricultural occupations, 21 (18.4 per cent) were ironstone miners and 46 (42 per cent) were coal miners. Besides Pilley Hills Colliery, the coal miners might also have been employed at Vizard's Colliery, two miles to the east in Hoyland or in the collieries worked by Newton Chambers at Thorncliffe, two miles to the south.

Wharncliffe Silkstone Colliery was sunk in 1853–54, its name being formed from the landowner, the Earl of Wharncliffe, of Wortley Hall, under whose property the mining was to take place and the Silkstone Seam, a very important house and coking coal, was the first coal seam to be worked. The company, the Wharncliffe Silkstone Colliery Company, was at first headed by Robert Baxter, George Blake Walker, and they were joined by Edmund Baxter, Horace Walker and John Jeffcock. The sinking of the colliery was supervised by the engineering consultants Woodhouse & Jeffcock, one of the partners of the concern being Parkin Jeffcock, John Jeffcock's son. Parkin Jeffcock lost his life in 1866 at the Oaks Colliery disaster in Barnsley. The same company managed the colliery until nationalisation in 1947. The colliery became well known locally and nationally because of the very early technical and safety innovations (e.g. coal cutters, conveyors and breathing apparatus) installed there, because they had a very early rescue station and the first checkweighman (a person elected by the miners to check the accuracy of the amount of coal mined recorded by the colliery company's weighman) in the whole country. The colliery operated for over a century during which time seven seams were worked. In 1918 it employed more than 1,500 men and boys. It eventually closed in 1966.

The first edition Six-inch Ordnance Survey map was published in 1855, just one year after the opening of Wharncliffe Silkstone Colliery and illustrates clearly the settlement on the brink of a new era. Pilley itself was then a small linear hamlet extending for about 300 yards from the *Gate Inn* in the north to the junction of Lidgett Lane and the northern end of Pilley Green. Three hundred yards further south at the southern end of Pilley Green there was another small cluster of buildings, just before Carr Lane and New Road were reached. To the south of Carr Lane agricultural land in the shape of tree-lined small fields stretched for another 300 yards towards the South Yorkshire Railway beside which stood the new Wharncliffe Silkstone Colliery. At the colliery a very short mineral railway connecting with the main railway line is shown, together with an engine house, a smithy, a pump, and three very short rows of buildings that may be cottages.

Fifty years later the 25-inch Ordnance survey, map published in 1905, shows that Pilley had been transformed (Figure 5.1). But this was almost entirely by peripheral growth from the northern end of Pilley Green to the colliery, a distance of half a mile, making the 'joined-up' settlement a winding three-quarters of a mile long from the *Gate Inn* in the north to the pit yard in the south. In the new colliery company, land owner-built extension were more than 150 residential dwellings, including about 130 in the pit yard. These included Hut Square, about two dozen small cottages grouped on four sides of a small square, Post Office Row, and the Stone Rows, two rows, one of eight cottages and the other of 18 cottages. The Hut Square cottages were no more than 100 yards from a pit shaft and the Stone Rows were between 35 and 70 yards from the coke ovens. In 1886 the colliery company built Wharncliffe Silkstone Club and Reading Room in the pit yard. One room, which became known as the Guild Room, was made available for the vicar's wife to hold sewing meetings with miners' wives. A prefabricated building was also erected as a gymnasium. Outside the pit yard to the north of New Road/Carr Lane were more substantial houses for senior colliery officials. The most splendid of these were 18 semi-detached houses built in 1901, black and white 'half-timbered', with long front gardens (see inset in Figure 5.1). Finally at the northern end of Pilley Green was the Mission Church (which in its early days was also used as a day school), built in 1871 by the Earl of Wharncliffe, and the parsonage. Another

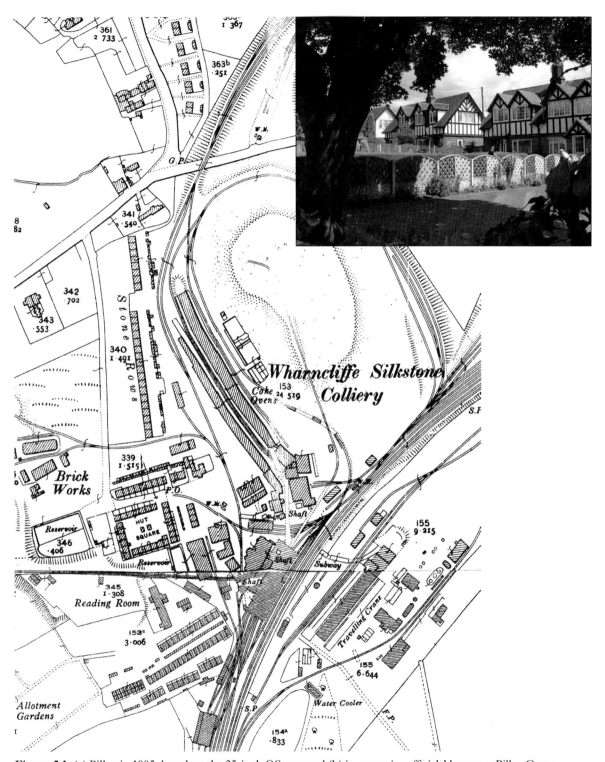

Figure 5.1 (a) Pilley in 1905, based on the 25-inch OS map and (b) inset: senior officials' houses at Pilley Green.

innovation was the building of an isolation hospital about half a mile from the pit yard because of the prevalence of smallpox, but it was never used for this purpose.

According to the 1901 census returns there were 127 occupied and three unoccupied houses in the pit yard housing a population of 720 men, women and children. These included 260 working men and boys of whom 243 (93.5 per cent) worked at the colliery. These included a great variety of specialized occupations including colliery engineers, colliery clerks, a colliery shaft inspector, deputies, hewers, rippers, trammers and pony boys. There were also four retired miners and one retired miner 'now artist'. Those not employed at the colliery included the steward at the club, a police constable and one man who worked at the hospital. There were also two men, both boarders, who had been born in Ireland, who were described as 'cattlemen on a farm'. Only three women were given occupations: one was sub-postmistress, another (a daughter) was a school teacher and the third was the wife of the retired miner who was now an artist, who was said to 'bake and sell bread'.

What must not be forgotten is that in 1901 when the census was taken, Wharncliffe Silkstone Colliery had been in operation for nearly half a century. It was therefore a far more settled community than some of the colliery settlements further east that at that time were only a few years old. It is not surprising then that in 1901 more than 40 per cent of the working men and boys had been born in Tankersley or the neighbouring townships of Hoyland and Worsbrough (which included Birdwell) and that if the catchment area is widened to the whole of South Yorkshire the figure rises to 70 per cent. There were also good numbers of medium and long distance migrants who had been living in Pilley for such a length of time that they had working sons born in Tankersley. For example, a horsekeeper at the colliery who had been born in Chedburgh in Suffolk had three sons all born in Tankersley and working at the pit, and a retired miner who had been born in Staveley in Derbyshire had seven sons working at the pit all of whom had been born in Tankersley. That being said there were people living in Pilley in 1901 from counties as far apart as Northumberland and Durham in the north and Wiltshire and Somerset in the south.

In 1901, just outside the pit yard, were two cottages. One, Rothwell Cottage, was occupied by the colliery manager, Jonathan Wroe, born in neighbouring Birdwell and the other, Sommeroaks Cottage, was the home of colliery under-manager Henry Cooper, born in Alfreton in Derbyshire. To the north along Pilley Green, the new colliery houses along the eastern side must still have been under construction but along the western side there were twelve cottages. In six of these the head of household was employed by the colliery. Other occupations of heads of household included a shop manager, a cordwainer and a carriage proprietor. One of those employed by the colliery was 59-year-old Jabez Wadsworth, who as a nine-year-old had worked as a gin boy (working with a pony to wind the ore and the workers up and down a bell pit) at the ironstone mines in Tankersley Park in 1851.

The shape of Pilley, including the pit yard community, began to change again in the late 1930s as the old cottages in the pit yard were condemned and a new council estate was built between the village street (Chapel Road) and Pilley Lane. Today there is new housing in the heart of old Pilley but the *Gate Inn* has been demolished. The colliery site itself, including the site of the miners' cottages in the pit yard, was landscaped following the closure of the colliery in 1966 and most of the site became the Wentworth Industrial Park located in a prime position close to junction 36 of the M1 motorway.

Kilnhurst

Kilnhurst has a long and interesting industrial history. The name itself, first recorded in the early fourteenth century, is derived from the Old English *cyln-hurst* meaning a wooded hill with a kiln. This may mean it had an early pottery industry. By the mid-eighteenth century there were certainly two potteries there and the first edition OS Six-Inch map published in 1855 shows Kilnhurst Pottery (earthenware) located next to the Sheffield & South Yorkshire Navigation. By the second half of the eighteenth century, the 2nd Marquis of Rockingham of Wentworth Woodhouse had a wharf at Kilnhurst on the River Don from where he transported coal from his Low Wood Colliery which worked the Barnsley Seam in Wentworth and Brampton townships. The coal reached markets on the lower Don in South Yorkshire and in north Nottinghamshire and north Lincolnshire. By the mid-nineteenth century a long mineral railway ran from Rawmarsh Colliery for more than a mile to the canal at Kilnhurst. There was also a forge at Kilnhurst Bridge. But at this time the settlement was still very small and was concentrated near the forge and at the eastern end of what became Victoria Street.

By the turn of the twentieth century great changes had occurred. Thrybergh Hall Colliery had been sunk in the late 1850s between the Midland Railway and the Sheffield & South Yorkshire Navigation next to Kilnhurst Pottery. To the north-east of the colliery was a substantial brickworks and north of the colliery there was a saw mill and the Victoria Glass Works. Kilnhurst Forge was still in operation and north of the settlement beside the Great Central Railway was the Queen's Foundry.

Kilnhurst Colliery, called Thrybergh Hall Colliery until the early 1920s, was sunk in 1858 by J. & J. Charlesworth of Wakefield. Located as it was next to the Sheffield & South Yorkshire Navigation canal, coal was at first transported mainly by canal down to the Humber ports. But faster distribution of coal and coke was soon undertaken on the Midland Railway that ran just to the west of the colliery and on the Great Central Railway just to the east, to both of which it was connected by short mineral railways. In 1923 the colliery became the property of Stewarts & Lloyds and coke was supplied to their iron and steels works at Corby in Northamptonshire and in the West Midlands. In 1936 the colliery changed hands once again, becoming the property of Tinsley Park Colliery Company but this lasted only until 1945 when it was acquired by the United Steel Company until nationalisation in 1947. Then in 1949, after nationalisation, it was linked into one combined colliery, coke and by-products complex with Manvers Main Colliery,

Wath Main Colliery and Barnburgh Main Colliery. Wath and Kilnhurst were linked underground with Manvers. Finally, in 1986, Manvers, Wath and Kilnhurst merged to form what was known as the Manvers Complex. But the Complex was finally closed in 1988. Over the 130 years of its life five seams were worked: High Hazel, Barnsley, Haigh Moor, Parkgate and Silkstone.

The industrial expansion resulted in much house building and settlement expansion. By the time of the 1901 census, on both sides of Hooton Road between the forge and the *Ship Inn* on the bank of the canal, were long terraced rows and leading off from the road at its western end were two long terraced streets, Thomas Street and Charles Street. Victoria Street extended westwards from the *Ship Inn* to the bridge over the Midland Railway and was now the main focus of the town with important public buildings (a National School built in 1872 on a site given by Thomas Gray Fullerton of Thrybergh Hall and a Board School erected in 1879, a United Free Methodist Chapel and a Primitive Methodist Chapel), on the road itself and short terraced rows running off it to the south (Figure 5.2). On Victoria Street itself, according to the Sheffield & Rotherham Directory for 1902, lived a surgeon, and various businesses including a fried fish dealer, several butchers and grocers, a chemist, a newsagent and tobacconist, a hairdresser, a picture framer, a draper & bootmaker and a dressmaker. Beyond the end of Victoria Street on Wentworth Road the settlement snaked westwards for more than another mile. First was St Thomas' Anglican church, erected in 1858–59, surrounded by its graveyard, and the vicarage built in 1860, both mostly at the expense of Earl Fitzwilliam. Beyond the vicarage was the small outlier of Albany Row and a good quarter of a mile beyond that was the bigger outlier of Piccadilly.

Despite the presence of a range of industrial employers, within two decades of the opening of Thrybergh Hall Colliery, Kilnhurst was well and truly a mining village as reflected in the occupations of men and boys in the 1901 census. This is well illustrated in an analysis of the census returns for 1901 for just two streets. Charles Street was one of two long streets of terraced houses leading off from Hooton Road between the River Don and the Great Central Railway. It contained 60 households in which lived 120 employed men and boys. Of these, 84 (70 per cent) were employed at the colliery, ranging from a pit deputy down to a pony driver and lamp cleaner. Nine were employed in the glassworks and two in the pottery. The men and boys living in Charles Street were predominantly locally born, with 42 (35 per cent) born in Kilnhurst itself, 37 (31 per cent) from other places in South Yorkshire and a further 16 (13 per cent) born elsewhere in Yorkshire. Most other migrants were either from the neighbouring counties of Lincolnshire, Nottinghamshire and Derbyshire or from the West Midlands. Even more predominantly occupied by colliery employees was Wentworth Terrace at the outlying settlement of Piccadilly. In Wentworth Terrace in 1901 lived 58 employed men and boys of whom 46 (79 per cent) were colliers. Seventy-one per cent (41) had been born either in Kilnhurst or neighbouring South Yorkshire settlements.

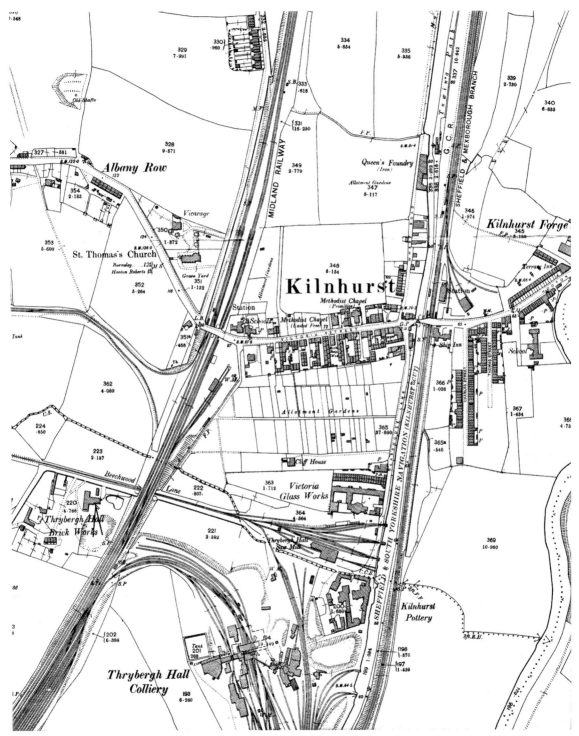

Figure 5.2 Kilnhurst as shown on the 25-inch OS map published in 1903. The colliery was just to the south of the village.

High Green

High Green, as its name suggests, started life as a tiny rural hamlet, around a small green. Nearby were two other hamlets, Potter Hill and Mortomley, both of which eventually merged with High Green. High Green began to grow and change its function after 1793 with the establishment of Newton Chambers' Thorncliffe Ironworks in the Blackburn Brook valley to the east. But more than 150 years earlier in John Harrison's survey of the Manor of Sheffield in 1637 four 'Coale pitts' were recorded in the fields between High Green and Mortomley.

Newton Chambers' ironworks not only provided employment in the works but also in local ironstone pits and collieries to supply the raw material and the fuel for the works' blast furnaces and foundries. Ironstone mining, from shallow bell pits, went on until about 1880 and the last coal from the nearby former Newton Chambers colliery, the Thorncliffe Drift, which had been opened in 1859, was hauled to the surface in 1955. Until it was developed for housing in the 1990s, the large area to the north of High Green called Foster Ground, was peppered with old ironstone bell pit mounds, as was the gently sloping valley side down to the Thorncliffe Ironworks between Mortomley and Lane End. Besides Thorncliffe Colliery, Newton Chambers also owned in the nineteenth century, within walking distance of High Green, Newbiggin Colliery, Westwood Colliery, Norfolk Colliery and Tankersley Colliery.

In 1841 the population of High Green and Mortomley was 905. The working population amounted to 292 of whom 121 (41.4 per cent) were either coal or ironstone miners. By 1871 the population had grown by nearly 300 per cent in just 30 years to 2,581, with 60 per cent of all employed males described in the census as either miner, collier, coal miner or ironstone miner. And the population was very youthful with nearly 40 per cent of the population under 15 years of age and only six per cent over 60. And there were many short-distance migrants. Because the enumerators put 'Ecclesfield' as the birthplace of the locally-born inhabitants it is assumed that this refers to anyone born within the large parish of Ecclesfield (including High Green) so that it is not possible to distinguish between High Green-born and other local migrants. Having said that, the vast majority, 1,939, were born within ten miles of High Green in 1871 and a further 189 were born in other parts of Yorkshire. The neighbouring counties of Derbyshire (90), Lancashire (42), Lincolnshire (34) and Nottinghamshire (27) also supplied substantial numbers of migrants as did the midland counties of Leicestershire (60) and Staffordshire (30). Altogether there were migrants who had been born in 30 English counties together with Scotland and Wales. There were also 47 Irish-born migrants living in the village. The number of Irish-born migrants living in High Green and Mortomley and in the nearby Westwood Rows (see Chapter2), together with their English-born offspring led to the building of a Roman Catholic church and school at Mortomley in 1886. A new church separate from the school was opened in 1907. This school complemented the existing High Green School and a mechanics institute opened in 1843 as both a day school and an evening school for 'youths engaged as miners and artisans'.

The impact of all this migration and population growth was the merging of High Green with Potter Hill, Thompson Hill and Mortomley through the erection of short terraced rows beside or running away from Wortley Road, the main street running through the village (Figure 5.3). For example, at Piece End there were six short terraces containing 63 households. In 1881 Piece End was the home of 367 people and 103 (78 per cent) of all the men and boys employed were miners. The nearby New Street consisted of two rows of five houses on each side of the street (Figure 5.4). Jean Huddlestone, born in 1923, from the nearby hamlet of Howbrook, used to have lunch in a house in New Street every day during the school week in the second half of the 1920s and early 1930s. Writing in her memoirs published in 1995 she wrote of New Street:

New Street… was directly opposite the school gates, the street where the candy man stopped his cart. 'New' it must have been once but there was nothing very new looking about the rows of terraced houses. The front windows were tidily curtained, the steps and windowsills whitened. The Coltons lived in the one next to the end in the first block. Afterwards came a ginnel and the

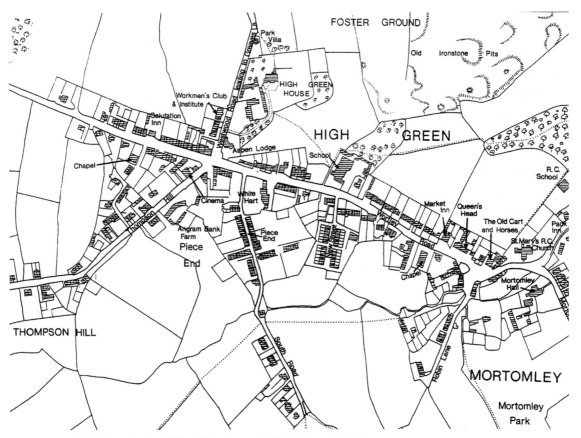

Figure 5.3 High Green in the 1920s. (*Chapeltown & High Green Archive*)

beginning of another block. Beyond that were allotments and the Miners' Welfare Hall. The front doors were seldom used except for funerals when the coffin could be brought straight downstairs and through the door and consequently the street looked shut up and tidy. All the life went on at the back where there was a rough patch of grass for washing lines and a cinder path. Each house had its small back yard paved with brick and with coalplace, washhouse and lavatory side by side at the bottom opposite the back door. These lavatories were always the same; white-washed walls, white-wood seat, high cistern and long chain to pull, squares of newspaper hanging on a string behind the door and darkness when the door was shut.

It was a poor house – I can see that now – but they received me into it and cherished me with such warm and unobtrusive friendliness that it was a rich place.

But it was not only the miners who lived in nineteenth century High Green and Mortomley. Mr George Chambers, a colliery owner, lived at High Green House from the mid 1840s until the 1870s and Mortomley Hall was the property of John and Catherine (née Parkin) Jeffcock of Cowley Manor, Chapeltown. St Saviour's Anglican church was built in 1872 in memory of their son, Parkin Jeffcock, the mining engineer, who lost his life attempting to free trapped miners in the Oaks Colliery disaster at Barnsley in 1866. At the laying of the foundation stone, Dr Gatty, vicar of Ecclesfield, said that Jeffcock was 'the collier's friend'.

Figure 5.4 New Street High Green. (*Chapeltown & High Green Archive*)

A former resident of High Green, now in his 90s recalled his abiding memories of High Green when he was growing up there in the 1930s: '…I think of the coal allowances dumped in the front gardens of the cottages below Mr Cottam's waiting to be barrowed or bucketed through to the back of the houses, or miners squatting on their heels against the Co-op wall waiting for the pit bus to carry them to their shift…'. Such scenes are no more. Today the site of Thorncliffe Colliery has been landscaped and is part of an industrial estate, the site of the large spoil heap that once stood beside the Westwood Rows has been landscaped and now forms part of Westwood Country Park, there is no sign of Newbiggin Colliery, the spoil of Norfolk Colliery lies hidden in Parkin Wood and the Foster Ground ironstone pits lie under modern housing. High Green today is simply a northern residential suburb of the city of Sheffield.

Treeton

In 1819 in his *History of Hallamshire*, Joseph Hunter, the father of South Yorkshire local history, stated that Treeton 'stands in a retired and pleasant situation, no turnpike road passing through it. The inhabitants for the most part are employed in agriculture'. He might also have added that the village was built largely of rose-pink Mexborough ('Rotherham Red') Rock with thatched roofs adding to its rustic character. The village was dominated by its church, whose solid stone tower jutted up above the rest of the village.

But this rural face was soon to change forever. In 1840 Treeton entered the railway age when George Stephenson brought the North Midland Railway through the eastern part of the township on the edge of the River Rother floodplain. Then, inevitably, at the beginning of the next decade came the first of a number of important colliery developments to exploit the rich Barnsley and Silkstone coal seams that lay beneath Treeton and the surrounding area.

Orgreave Colliery was sunk in 1851 just less than half a mile to the south-west of the village. Then, in 1863, the Fence Colliery Company sank the Fence Colliery, about a mile and a half south of Treeton down to the Barnsley seam at 154 yards. This company then acquired the Orgreave Colliery from the Sorby family in 1870 and suspended production there in 1871–72 to allow for major expansion and redevelopment. The company was then reconstituted in 1874 as Rothervale Collieries Limited with a lease of 2,865 acres of land from the Duke of Norfolk under which they would mine for coal. In the following year work started on the sinking of Treeton Colliery.

The first sod was cut at the sinking of Treeton Colliery on 13 October 1875. The *Rotherham Advertiser* reported that 'The sun shone brilliantly and the charming landscape which was soon to be disfigured by colliery headgear and huge chimneys was the subject of much admiration.' The Barnsley Seam was reached in early 1878 but the bad state of the coal trade and lack of capital caused a closure from September 1878 until the spring of 1882. Soon Treeton was not dominated by its medieval parish church but by Treeton Colliery with its pithead buildings, coal washery plant, reservoir, a large and growing pit heap, and clay pit and brickworks.

The population of Treeton grew quickly. It was 383 in 1871, had more than doubled by 1881 and by 1901 had more than doubled again to 1,979. To accommodate this rapidly growing population the colliery company built about 234 cottages in Treeton. These were in four 'ribbons', extending out of the existing village – one on Mill Lane to the west, one along Treeton Wood Lane to the east and two northwards along Well Lane at Bole Hill Row and New Bole Hill. The quarries at Bole Hill provided the stone for more than 100 of these cottages, the rest being built of brick (Figure 5.5).

The 1901 census reveals a village populated overwhelmingly by families whose menfolk were employed at the local collieries (Treeton Colliery in 1908 employed 1091 underground and 273 on the surface) and these families were predominantly headed by someone born outside the village. Take Mill Lane for example. On Mill Lane in 1901 there were 50 purpose-built miners' cottages. These houses contained 136 employed men and boys. These included not only father and son or

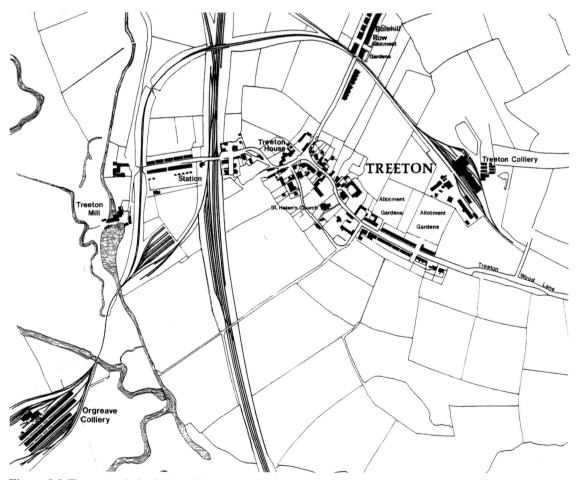

Figure 5.5 Treeton at the beginning of the twentieth century based on the 25-inch OS map published in 1903.

sons, but also families with single men boarding with them. And of these 136 men and boys, 129 (95 per cent) were colliery workers, from pit deputies down to pit pony drivers. The seven not employed at the pits were two grocers, a painter, a stone mason, a wood sawyer, a groom and one old man living on his own means. What is even more staggering is that only 12 (8.8 per cent) of these 136 men and boys were born in the village. Thirty-four (25 per cent) were born in other places in South Yorkshire, a mixture of neighbouring towns, other mining villages and rural settlements. Other parts of Yorkshire and the neighbouring counties of Lincolnshire, Nottinghamshire and Lancashire provided small numbers but Derbyshire was a substantial contributor with 33 (24 per cent), most of these originating in the north of the county. The West Midlands, as in many other South Yorkshire mining settlements, was the place of birth of a substantial number of incomers (23 men and boys [17 per cent.]). Men from Wales (six from Flintshire), Scotland (one, born in the small town of Stornoway on the Isle of Lewis in the Outer Hebrides) and Ireland (four) had made their way to a South Yorkshire mining village. The lure of a job in a coal mining village in the north of England had pulled one man from the village of Debden in Essex, another from the town of Lewes in Sussex and a third from Acton on the edge of London in Middlesex.

It was not just the mine labourers and their families who came to live in the village. There was, of course, a rector and a curate living in the Rectory and at Treeton House on Front Street lived two doctors, both described as surgeons and physicians, one born in Ireland and the other in Scotland. Men at all levels of colliery supervision and management also came to live in the village. The colliery houses on Treeton Wood Lane, for instance, included the 'Big Six' built for more senior men, and there were two specially-built detached houses, one for the pit manager and one for the engineer. John Howard Keep, the Secretary of Rothervale Collieries Limited was recorded in 1901 living at Treeton Hall with his two young sons (one born in Sydney, Australia), a nurse, housemaid and cook. In the same year Frederick John Jones, the Managing Director of the company was living at Treeton Grange which he had had built in the 1890s away from both the village and the pit. The household consisted of himself, his three sons and two daughters, ranging in age from 17 to 23, a female visitor and four servants. Jones served two terms as President of the Mining Association of Great Britain and in 1919 became Sir Frederick Jones.

A new Board School was opened in 1880 and extended in 1901–02, a Reading Room was opened in 1888, the parish church was fully restored in 1892, and in the same year a Wesleyan chapel was built. Treeton railway station on the Midland Railway line was opened in 1884. Perhaps the most notable development in the village in this period took place in 1897. In that year Treeton became the first village in England with electric street lighting, installed at a cost of £900. Significantly Frederick Jones, Managing Director of Rothervale Collieries Limited was Chairman of the new (1894) parish council and the electrical power was derived from the colliery company's dynamos.

In 1918 the Rothervale Collieries were amalgamated with the United Steel Company that retained ownership until nationalisation in 1947. Coal production at Treeton Colliery continued until 1990, the Wath Wood and Swallow Wood seams being exploited from the 1960s, having

Figure 5.6 (a) Pit Lane leading to Treeton Colliery with the men coming off shift (*Michael Bentley*) and (b) the colliery site today with its extensive new residential developments.

taken over from the exhausted Barnsley and Haigh Moor seams which had been exploited continuously from the late 1870s and 1880s respectively. The last coal was produced on 17 December 1990.

On 28 January 1994 it was reported in the the *Rotherham Advertiser* that after months of painstaking negotiations with the landowner (the Duke of Norfolk's estates), the general public and local organizations, Rotherham MBC Planning Committee had approved in principle the massive redevelopment of the site of Treeton Colliery. The main feature of the plan was to be the building of homes in a variety of sizes and styles from executive housing, down to starter homes and social housing built by housing associations. There was to be provision for new shops and an extension to the nearby school.

The redevelopment plan was put into action, the colliery site is now a residential extension to the old village (Figure 5.6) and together with housing development to the north and south of Station Road between the old village core and the railway, has transformed Treeton into a compact residential village, once more dominated not by colliery headgear and muck stack but by its medieval church tower. Treeton Grange is a private care home.

Darfield

The ancient village of Darfield lay on a low spur of Mexborough Rock in the Dearne valley overlooking low-lying land, Firth Ings to the east and Wombwell Ings to the south, both liable to floods in the past. By the second half of the nineteenth century the village nucleus was around the crossroads formed by the east-west running Church Street and the north-south running School Street and Vicar Road. Within this core were the ancient parish church, the rectory, the *Cross Keys Inn*, a school, a number of farms and the police station. The churchyard contains a monument to the 189 miners who lost their lives in the explosion at Lundhill Colliery in 1857 (see Chapter 2).

The sinking of Darfield Main Colliery, which was connected to the Great Central Railway main line by Darfield Main Siding, began in 1856 and the Barnsley Seam, seven feet and six inches thick here, was reached in the summer of 1860. In October 1872 a serious underground fire closed the colliery, which at the time employed between 400 and 500 men, for several months. The great rivalry between Darfield Main colliery and Mitchell Main Colliery, less than a mile to west, ended in the early 1900s when Darfield Main was bought by the Mitchell Main Colliery Company. A decision was then made to work the seams above the Barnsley Seam (which became exhausted in 1910) from Darfield Main and those below the Barnsley Seam from Mitchell Main. Modernization went on at Darfield Main throughout the twentieth century: a new shaft to the Thorncliffe Seam at 625 yards was opened in 1917; a long period of re-organization, modernization and replacement went on following nationalisation from 1948 to 1959; and between 1978 and the mid-1980s the workings were further deepened to the Silkstone Seam at 695 yards. In 1986 the colliery was merged with Houghton Main Colliery to the north and finally closed in 1989.

The development of coal mining in the second half of the nineteenth century had a marked impact on population growth and its distribution. In 1841 the population of Darfield township was a mere 648, but had grown to 3,410 in 1891 and to 5,427 by 1911. By 1951 its population was 6,237. The population growth stimulated rapid settlement expansion. Darfield expanded northwards as reflected in the street names (Victoria Street, Queen Street, Coronation Street) and westwards along Barnsley Road and New Street to Snape Hill which formed an extension almost as big as the original village, and then on with small breaks to new additions at Low Valley, Elliott's Terrace, Cockstool Bridge and along Station Road into Wombwell. A major influence on the growth of Snape Hill and Low Valley as new mining settlements was the Hammerton family. Daniel Hammerton was a cabinet maker, upholsterer, general house furnisher and funeral director with premises at Snape Hill. A member of the Hammerton family was also surveyor and sanitary inspector for the urban district council. Between 1877 and 1894 Daniel Hammerton and a relative, Joseph Hammerton, submitted plans for the construction of 89 houses in the two settlements. Snape Hill also grew as a retail shopping and business centre and along Snape Hill Road. (Figure 5.7). In addition to Hammerton's shop and workshop, were a public house (the *Victoria Inn*), joiners and wide variety of shops including grocers, greengrocers, boot makers and dealers, butchers, a draper, a hairdresser and branch No 19 of the Barnsley British Co-operative Society.

Figure 5.7 Snape Hill, Darfield. (*Old Barnsley*)

And as in all the other coal mining settlements on the exposed coalfield, this population growth and settlement expansion had been fuelled by large-scale in-migration from places outside the immediate area. In 1841, for example, nearly two decades before the opening of Darfield Main Colliery, only 24 people out of the population of 648 (3.7 per cent) living in Darfield township had been born outside the West Riding of Yorkshire. By 1871, eleven years after the opening of Darfield Main, there were some dramatic changes. The original village of Darfield had only grown from 648 to 708, but its character was changing with now more than 20 per cent of its population born outside Yorkshire. At Snape Hill, however, the new settlement to the west of the old village, there was now a mining settlement with a population 294 with a third of them having been born outside Yorkshire and with 50 of them having been born in the West Midlands counties of Shropshire, Staffordshire, Warwickshire and Worcestershire. Even more significant were the changes taking place at Low Valley. This new settlement had grown nearly fivefold from 139 to 661 between 1861 and 1871 and most of its inhabitants (53 per cent) had been born outside Yorkshire. The main birthplaces of its migrant population were the West Midlands counties (142 persons or 21.2 per cent of the population), the neighbouring counties of Derbyshire and Nottinghamshire (59 persons or 8.6 per cent of the population) and Ireland (31 persons or 4.7 per cent of the population).

Royston

Royston, like Darfield, evolved from a stone-built rural village into an enlarged mining community in its early years, through expansion mainly in one direction rather than general enlargement. Until the coming of coal mining Royston was what is known by geographers as a 'street village', i.e. it stretched from west to east along High Street (with some development behind High Street on Back Lane and Occupation Lane) and then south-eastwards along Church Street past Royston Green (with its pinfold in which straying farm animals would be penned) on the right to the parish church towards the far end. There was also a little development to the north-east of High Street along Senior Lane (later re-named as Midland Road, see below). There was also a very small detached settlement beside the Barnsley Canal, opened in 1799) at Royston Bridge, including *The Ship* and *The Anchor* public houses that served the passing boat trade. Dominating the village for centuries, before the appearance of colliery headgear, would have been the tower of St John's parish church, built in the Perpendicular style in the fifteenth century. This church originally served the population of the very large parish of Royston which included not only the village of Royston, but also Carlton, Notton, Chevet, Monk Bretton, Cudworth and Woolley. Another unusual feature of the pre-industrial village was the unusually large number of orchards and gardens that are shown on the first edition Six-Inch Ordnance Survey map that was surveyed in 1849–51. These were market gardens.

The population of Royston at the time of the first national census in 1801 was 360. By 1851 it had grown to 587 and on the eve of the sinking of the colliery in 1871 it was 676. The long-established seasonal rural rhythm of this small agricultural village was changed following the registering of the Monckton Main Coal Company on 16 September 1874. The first sod was cut by the 6th Viscount Galway of Serlby Hall, north Nottinghamshire, chairman of the company, on 24 May 1875. Monckton, the name of the new colliery, was one of the family names of Viscount Galway. The 6th Viscount died later that year and he was succeeded by his son, the 7th Viscount, who remained chairman for over half a century. Production of coal from the Barnsley Seam started in 1878 and the following year the first coke ovens came into production. By about 1890 there were more than 150 coke ovens in production. In 1901 the original colliery company was wound up and a new company, New Monckton Collieries Limited, was incorporated. Modernization of both the colliery and the coke ovens went on throughout the first half of the twentieth century before and after nationalisation and was not finally completed until 1959, by which time there were six shafts in operation exploiting not only the Barnsley Seam but also Meltonfield, Beamshaw, Kent and Haigh Moor. The colliery closed in December 1966, at which time it employed more than 2,200 men, but the associated Monckton Coke and Chemical Works remained open until December 2014 using coal transported to it from elsewhere. One hundred and thirty employees lost their jobs on its closure in 2014.

Monckton Main was sunk on farmland between the Barnsley Canal and the Midland Railway in the west and Lundhill Lane in the east, almost a mile from the centre of the old village. As might be expected, the effect was to cause the creation of an ever-expanding 'adjunct' of brick-built housing development between the old village and the colliery to accommodate migrant miners and their families. The opening of the colliery caused a population explosion The population almost doubled between 1871 and 1881, from 676 to 1,128. By 1911 it had grown to 6,237 when there were 2,214 employed men living in Royston of whom 1,619 were employed in coal mining. Figure 5.8, which is based on a fieldwork survey carried out in 1959, shows the relationship between the old village nucleus and the colliery, with the nineteenth century largely brick-built adjunct that had developed between the two, together with later twentieth century development. Senior Lane between the old village and the colliery became Midland Road and developed as the main commercial thoroughfare with a wide range of shops and two cinemas (The Empire and the Palace). Today, more than 140 years after the cutting of the first sod at the colliery site, Royston is a suburban community of more than 9,000 people and the old spoil heaps now form Rabbit Ings Country Park.

A glimpse of the effect of more than two decades of the operation of the colliery and related coke ovens can be gained by analyzing the census data for 1901 for just one street that was developed after the sinking of the new colliery – Senior Lane which by 1901 was called Midland Road. In that year 81 employed men and boys were living on Midland Road of whom 68 (84 per cent) were working either at the colliery or the coke ovens. These ranged from a colliery manager and two by-product oven managers to a pit pony driver and a colliery lamp boy. There were also four grocers reflecting the growing business role of the main street through the new part of the village. The

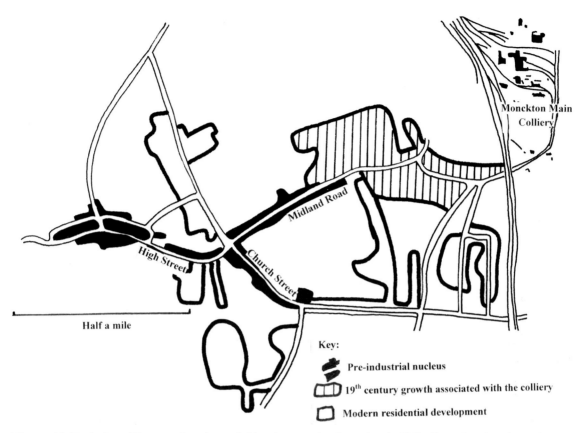

Figure 5.8 Evolution of Royston, based on a fieldwork survey by the author in 1959. Since that date the settlement has expanded in all directions, particularly to the west.

other striking feature about Midland Road in 1901 was that only eight of the 81 employed men and boys had been born in Royston. Twenty-five were from other parts of Yorkshire, both nearby and further afield (e.g. Castleford, Armley and Dewsbury in West Yorkshire and from Scampston in the then North Riding), and 48 (59 per cent) men and boys living in the road had been born in sixteen other English counties and in north and south Wales. Of the English counties, six were from Staffordshire and seven from Dudley just across the county boundary in Worcestershire – just a small number of the many 'Black Country' migrants who flocked to Royston.

Thurnscoe and Goldthorpe

It is worth considering these two settlements together, because of their proximity to each other. They began to be developed as mining communities within sixteen years of each other and much of the land on which they were developed was in the same ownership. And their histories are both linked inextricably to a third settlement, the neighbouring village of Hickleton.

On the eve of the sinking of Hickleton Main Colliery in 1892, Thurnscoe and Goldthorpe were small agricultural settlements in an area of rural England hardly touched by the Industrial Revolution. The only sign of modernity was the Midland & North Eastern Railway line that snaked across the countryside from south to north less than 200 yards to the west of Goldthorpe and about half a mile to the east of the centre of Thurnscoe. Thurnscoe was a small rural village dominated by the eighteenth-century tower of its church and separated by hedged fields from Thurnscoe Hall set in its small park to the east of the village. To the south Goldthorpe was no more than a hamlet without a church or chapel. Lying less than a mile to the east lay Hickleton, a small estate village with a Perpendicular church and Hickleton Hall, a Georgian country house, set in its landscaped park. This was the home of the 2nd Viscount Halifax (1839–1934) that was inherited by his son, Earl Halifax, who was Viceroy of India from 1926 to 1929 and Foreign Secretary from 1938 to 1940. It was largely under their land that the seams worked by Hickleton Main Colliery and Goldthorpe Colliery lay. For more than half a century, until nationalisation, they would benefit from the income from the lease of their land and the royalties from the production of coal while Hickleton would remain a small village untouched by industrialization and Thurnscoe and Goldthorpe would be changed out of all recognition (Figure 5.9).

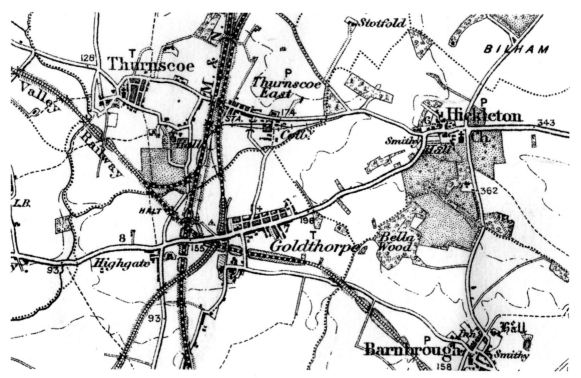

Figure 5.9 Thurnscoe and Goldthorpe in the early stages of change from agricultural to mining settlements as shown on the One Inch OS map (enlarged) published in 1908. To the east Hickleton remains unchanged.

The sinking of Hickleton Main Colliery by Hickleton Main Colliery Company just to the east of Thurnscoe began in 1892 and the Barnsley Seam was reached in 1894. This was a very large colliery employing more than a thousand men by the 1890s. Besides the Barnsley Seam, five other seams were exploited. From 1986 the colliery was only operational on a care and maintenance basis and finally closed in 1988. Goldthorpe Colliery, just to the east of Goldthorpe, about a mile south of Hickleton Main Colliery, was sunk in 1910 to work the Shafton Seam. The last coal was raised in 1994. A third colliery, Highgate Colliery, just to the west of Goldthorpe was sunk in 1916, also to work the Shafton Seam. In 1966 Goldthorpe and Highgate were connected underground. Highgate Colliery closed in 1985.

The population of Hickleton in 1801 was only 174 and a century later by 1901 was still only 178. By contrast, the population of Thurnscoe had grown by a staggering 1100 (eleven hundred) per cent between 1891 and 1901 from 217 to 2, 366. By 1921 Hickleton's population had declined to 138 while Thurnscoe's had grown to almost 5,000.

Hickleton Main Colliery was located about a mile and a quarter to the east of the old village of Thurnscoe beyond the railway just south of Lidget Lane about a mile from Hickleton. It was connected to the railway network by a series of sidings and mineral lines. The miners at the colliery in the early days were, of course, mostly migrants. Housing for the miners and their families was built immediately to the west of the colliery in an area bounded by the railway in the west and Lidget Lane in the south. This became Thurnscoe East or *t'Top End* and the old

Figure 5.10 St John the Evangelist and St Mary Magdalene church, the concrete church, Goldthorpe. (*Old Barnsley*)

village became Old Thurnscoe or *t'Bottom End*. Goldthorpe just expanded outwards towards Thurnscoe to the north and Bolton upon Dearne to the south. It has already been pointed out that before the coming of the colliery Goldthorpe had neither church nor chapel. This was changed when between 1914 and 1916, St John the Evangelist and St Mary Magdalene church was built at the instigation and cost of the 2nd Viscount Halifax of Hickleton Hall on whose land the colliery and mining settlement were located and under whose land the coal was being mined. He commissioned Alfred Nutt to design the church which is made of concrete – Britain's first concrete church (Figure 5.10). It contains a stained glass window commemorating the miners who worked in local collieries for more than a century.

Both Thurnscoe and Goldthorpe continued to expand outwards during the second half of the twentieth century and now form one continuous built-up area stretching from Thurnscoe in the north to Goldthorpe and then to Bolton upon Dearne in the south, a distance of three miles. The site of Hickleton Main Colliery has been landscaped and now forms Phoenix Park incorporating Thurnscoe Community Woodland managed by the Forestry Commission. Part of the site of Goldthorpe Colliery is now covered by housing. The main industrial area now in Goldthorpe is Goldthorpe Industrial Estate.

Wath upon Dearne

Until the sinking of local collieries, Wath upon Dearne was a thriving agricultural village located on the edge of the floodplain of the River Dearne which flowed west to east, about two-thirds of a mile to the north of the village. The name Wath is the old Viking name for a ford across a river. The river was reached across damp meadowland formerly known as the Great Moor and Low Common. To the south of the village lay a rural landscape that once held the open medieval fields enclosed in the late eighteenth century and beyond those Boyd Royd Wood, a coppice wood, and beside it the former wooded common of Wath Wood. Detached from the village, to the west, was the smaller agricultural village of West Melton and to the south Newhill Hall, built in 1785 for the Payne family, successful farmers and tanners, set in its parkland. Although there was a scattering of coal pits throughout the area in the eighteenth and nineteenth centuries, they were small-scale and subsidiary to the agricultural economy.

The first intimations of the great change that was to come to disturb the quiet seasonal rural rhythm of life was the completion of the Dearne and Dove Canal between 1797 and 1804 that linked part of the exposed coalfield with the Don Navigation at Swinton. By 1820 100,000 tons of coal were being carried on the canal. Then in 1840 the Midland Railway linking Derby with Leeds was built across the Low Common and Great Moor, followed, just to the south of it, by the South Yorkshire Railway in 1849.

The small collieries in operation before 1870 mined the seams at shallow depths such as the Meltonfield Seam, but what the large coal owners were after was access to large areas of the deeper and eight feet thick Barnsley Seam. This saw the development of two new deep collieries in the vicinity of Wath. The first sod at Manvers Main No 1 Colliery was turned in 1867 and the Barnsley Seam was reached in 1870 at a depth of more than 280 yards when the first coal was raised to the surface. The colliery company was known as the Manvers Main Colliery Company because most of the land beneath which the mining was to take place was to the east and north-east and belonged to the Adwick estate of the third Earl Manvers whose home was not local but at Thoresby Hall, near Ollerton in Nottinghamshire. There were four shafts at Manvers Main. The first two shafts were sunk between the canal and the South Yorkshire Railway halfway between Wath and Mexbrough (Manvers No 1) and the other two shafts (Manvers No. 2) were to the north-west. Coke and coal by-products production began in 1878. By the early 1940s the Barnsley Seam was exhausted and the exploitation of other seams began.

While all these developments were taking place at Manvers Main, just over half a mile to the north-west on Great Moor between the Midland and South Yorkshire railways, a second colliery was being sunk and expanded. This was Wath Main Colliery where the first coal was raised to the surface in 1879.

Then in 1949, after nationalisation, Manvers Main Colliery was linked into one combined colliery, coke and by-products complex with Wath Main Colliery, Kilnhurst Colliery (a mile and a half to the south-east) and Barnburgh Main Colliery (a mile to the north-east) . Wath and Kilnhurst were linked underground with Manvers while Barnburgh coal was delivered to Manvers by rail. Between 1955 and 1956, a new central coal preparation plant, the biggest in Europe, came into operation. Finally, in 1986, Manvers, Wath and Kilnhurst merged to form what was known as the Manvers Complex. But the Complex was finally closed in 1988.

The impact of coal mining development on the flood plain to the north and east of the village and on the village itself was immense. On the floodplain itself the world was literally turned upside down. It was a landscape that for more than a century was dominated by colliery headgear, smoking chimneys, railway sidings, pit heaps, coal preparation plants, coke ovens, coal washeries and for the greater part of the period in question the constant noise and steam from steam locomotives handling the coal, coke and other by-products.

Altogether Manvers and Barnburgh (also owned by Manvers Main Colliery Company) in 1938 employed 5,000 men and employment was still as high as nearly 2,400 in 1981. Obviously not all the miners and surface workers at Manvers Main and Wath Main collieries lived in Wath: they would have walked or come by bus, pit paddy and latterly by car from surrounding settlements such as Bolton upon Dearne, Mexborough, Swinton, West Melton, Brampton, Wombwell and Darfield. But having said that, Wath's population grew rapidly from the 1870s onwards. In 1801 its population stood at 662 and by 1871 had grown to 2,023. Within ten years it had grown to 3,012 and by the end of the century was nearly 5,000.

The rapid population growth resulted in Wath expanding in all directions. By the beginning of the twentieth century Wath had expanded along Doncaster Road to the east towards the site of Manvers Main Colliery No. 1 pit where a mixture of short and long rows had been built at right angles between the road and the South Yorkshire Railway (Figure 5.11). New housing also extended southwards towards Newhill Hall and eastwards beyond the *George & Dragon* public house towards West Melton, where by the early twentieth century a grid-iron pattern of streets had appeared north of the junction between High Street and Barnsley Road. Eventually with the expansion of Wombwell and Brampton to the west and Mexborough to the east an almost continuous ribbon of urban and semi-urban development would run for more than seven miles along the Dearne valley.

Like all other South Yorkshire mining settlements, Wath attracted migrants from all over the country - and beyond. This can be illustrated by analyzing the census returns for 1901 for just two streets within the village. The first is Chapel Street which extends south from Church Street in the centre of the village. This street in 1901 contained a complete social cross-section of the community. There were 99 employed males living in the street in that year and 47 of them were employed in some capacity in the local collieries from a colliery manager, colliery under-manager and coal inspector to a coal hewer, coal miner's lamp cleaner and coal miner's pick sharpener.

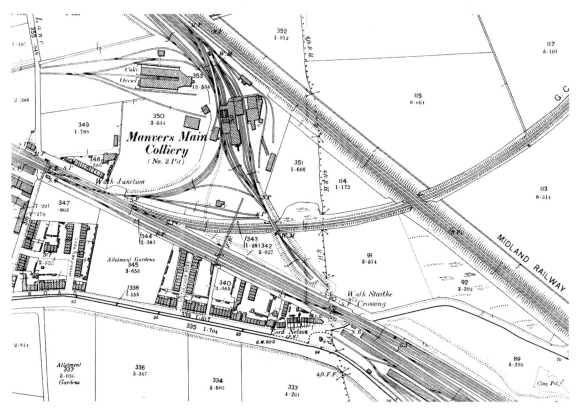

Figure 5.11 Manvers Main (no 2 pit) and to the south part of the outward expansion of Wath upon Dearne in the form of terraced rows for mining families as shown on the 25-inch OS map in 1901.

But also living amongst them was a surgeon, assistant surgeon, and an estate and house agent together with a range of tradesmen from a barber to a pork butcher and greengrocer. Forty-one of the 99 employed males had been born in Wath and 24 in other parts of South Yorkshire but the remaining 31 were from much further afield including other parts of Yorkshire, the neighbouring counties of Derbyshire, Nottinghamshire and Lincolnshire, the West Midlands, Northumberland in the north-east, Essex in the south-east, two from Scotland, two from Wales and one from Ireland. There was even a 27-year-old migrant, a general labourer, who had been born in Pietermaritzburg in South Africa!

Winifred Road was one of the streets of terrace houses erected between Doncaster Road and the railway line immediately to the south of Manvers No. 2 pit. Living along this street in 1901 were 44 employed males of whom 24 were employed in coal mining. The other men and boys were in a wide variety of occupations including a plate layer, a worker at a sewage farm, a glass blower and a labourer in a soap works. Only eight of the 44 had been born in Wath. Nine had been born in other parts of South Yorkshire and six from other parts of Yorkshire. The others came from widely different parts of the country including Northamptonshire, Rutland, Sussex, Scotland and Guernsey.

Manvers and Wath collieries, their coke ovens and by-product plants, their pit heaps, railway sidings and marshalling yards have now disappeared. Having lain derelict for more than half a decade until the mid-1990s, the whole area once devoted to mining and preparing and transporting coal products has now been reclaimed and landscaped with assistance from the European Social Fund and is now the site of extensive industrial warehousing, light industry, office space and residential development in a lakeside setting. The area also includes the RSPB Old Moor Wetland Centre, a 250-acre nature reserve designed by the Wildlife and Wetlands Trust.

Cudworth

Cudworth is interesting because it did not have a colliery. The coal miners living there had to travel out of their village to their work. Within a short distance to the south-west was Monk Bretton Colliery, opened in 1870 and closed in 1968, to the north-west was Wharncliffe Woodmoor 4 & 5 Colliery (New Carlton) that opened in 1876 and closed in 1970; and to the east was Grimethorpe Colliery, opened in 1897 and closed in 1992. There was also a bleachworks to the west of the settlement that operated from 1855 until about 1900.

Before the sinking of Monk Bretton and New Carlton collieries in the 1870s Cudworth comprised two separate small hamlets, Upper Cudworth in the north along the former turnpike road from Barnsley to Pontefract and Lower Cudworth in the south with its Manor House, Manor Farm and with part of the settlement around a former village green. By 1890 Upper Cudworth had expanded as far south as the *Star Inn* at the junction of Low Town Lane and Barnsley Road. But by 1904 there had been much more expansion in Upper Cudworth which by that date had extended northwards and southwards and almost merged with Lower Cudworth. Long terraced rows had appeared surrounded by allotments all along the main street (Barnsley Road) of Upper Cudworth and behind the main street, for example along Saville Street and Market Street in the north and along York Street and Somerset Street in the south. And along Burton Lane halfway between the village and Monk Bretton Colliery was the outlying residential area, made up of six short terraces in the form of a rectangle called Klondyke (see Chapter 3). By 1893 Cudworth also had its own Anglican church, St John the Baptist's.

These settlement changes are reflected in the population levels. In 1801 the combined population of Upper and Lower Cudworth was a mere 296 and it had only grown to 657 seventy years later in 1871. But with a colliery opening a short distance to the south-west in 1870 and to the north-west in 1876, the population rose to 1,044 in 1881 and by 1901, four years after the opening of Grimethorpe Colliery to the east, it was 3,400. The population of Cudworth continued to grow rapidly in the twentieth century reaching 6,824 in 1911 and by 1951, 8,763. It now has a population of just under 11,000.

Dinnington

Dinnington Main Colliery, like the one at Thurcroft (see Chapter 6) lay on the very eastern edge of the exposed coalfield and the old village of Dinnington just to the east, actually straddled the outcrop of the Magnesian Limestone that marked the boundary between the exposed and concealed coalfields.

Close inspection of the 25-Inch Ordnance Survey map of Dinnington surveyed just a few years before the sinking of the colliery reveals a picture of rural tranquillity as far removed as can be imagined from the villages to the west that had been industrialized in the previous half century. Here was a small nucleated village clustered around what must once have been a village green and dominated by St Leonard's church, a rectory and the *Falcon Inn*. In the 1850s, a Wesleyan chapel had been built on Barley Croft Lane on the northern edge of the village and in 1874 a small school was opened further along the same lane. Its first intake of pupils was just 38. On the western edge of the village the village pinfold was still in place and to the south an old windmill near North Anston still survived. And attached to the village on the south was Dinnington Hall, dating from the mid-eighteenth century, the home of the Althorpe family, set in its wooded park which still contained its fish pond and an icehouse.

Sinking of the colliery started in 1903 on land to the north-west of the old village between Outgang Lane in the north and Church Lane in the south. The colliery was served by the South Yorkshire Railway, a branch of the LMS and LNER. Production of coal from the Barnsley Seam began in 1906 and in the 1960s and 1970s the Swallow Wood and Haigh Moor seams also began to be exploited. Dinnington Main Colliery was owned until 1927 by a partnership between the Sheffield Coal Company and Sheepbridge Coal and Iron Company. After that date until nationalisation it became part of Yorkshire Amalgamated Collieries Ltd and then Amalgamated Denaby Collieries Limited. The coal was largely used for coke production, the first coke ovens coming into production in 1912. The colliery closed in 1991.

In 1901, five years before the colliery first came into production, the population of Dinnington was 250. Ten years later it had risen very sharply to almost 5,000. The first pit sinkers and miners lived in a temporary village (Tin Town) but very quickly the colliery company started to build housing on the edge of the existing village. By 1928 the area covered by the new colliery village covered a large area extending northwards for half a mile to Doe Quarry Lane and eastwards for half a mile between Doe Quarry Lane in the north and Swinston Hill Road in the south (Figure 5.12). The first streets were in form of terraced rows along Laughton Road at Leopold Street, on New Street (with fifteen short terraced rows running off to the north and south) and behind South Street. To the east of South Street fronting Laughton Road a detached and four semi-detached houses were also built presumably for senior colliery officials. Just before the junction of Laughton Road and Doe Quarry Lane there were five more terraced rows, one on Laughton Road itself and the others on Coronation Avenue and Plantation Avenue, the latter on the site of the old Tin Town. Terraces also soon appeared at the eastern end of Lorden's Hill.

Terrace housing extended eastwards from near the top of Laughton Road along Dinnington Terrace (believed to be the first permanent residential area in the village to house the population

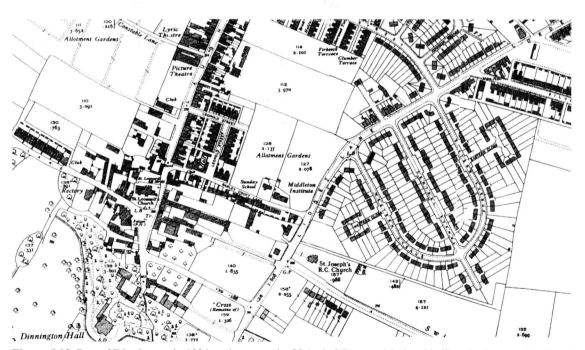

Figure 5.12 Part of Dinnington in 1926 as shown on the 25-inch OS map with the old village in the west, bordered on the east with the first mining village housing in the form of straight terraced rows and beyond those the curved avenues of later semi–detached housing.

of Tin Town), Doe Quarry Terrace and Recreation Terrace, Scarsdale Street and Victoria Street eventually joining up with the earlier terraced housing on the western side of Lorden's Hill and beyond on Leicester Road and Silverdales. Around every block of terraced housing were large areas of allotment gardens. In the period immediately after the First World War the village was extended further eastwards in the form of small estates of larger semi-detached houses with indoor toilets and front and back gardens. One of these was centred on the Crescent, another on Addison Square and a third around Western, Central and Eastern avenues. On the southern edge of the new colliery village substantial detached villas lined Swinston Hill Road by the end of the 1920s.

And it was not just housing development that had transformed Dinnington in the first thirty years of the twentieth century. At the top of Laughton Road a Wesleyan chapel and a new village school soon appeared. The Infants' Department opened in 1907 and the Mixed Department in 1908 when the 950-place school was fully subscribed. On Laughton Road a small public park was laid out with a bandstand in the middle. Across the road a miners' institute was built next to its football ground, cricket ground, running track, two bowling greens and tennis court. There were also a miners' welfare institute, bowling green and a tennis court on the eastern edge of the village. And Laughton Road which had become the main business thoroughfare boasted the Lyric Theatre, opened in 1910 and the Picture Palace, opened in 1913. Perhaps most importantly, in 1928, the Chelmsford Mining and Technical Institute (so-called because it was opened by Viscount Chelmsford, Chairman of the Miners' Welfare Central Committee), was opened to provide part-time and full-time courses in technical subjects related to the mining industry, other career related courses and WEA classes. It is now the Dinnington campus of Rotherham College of Arts and Technology.

Since the late 1920s Dinnington has grown outwards to the south and has now merged with North Anston. Many people now travel to work in Sheffield, Rotherham and Worksop. The colliery site has been levelled and now contains an industrial estate.

Chapter 6

New Mining Villages on the Exposed Coalfield

What is meant by a 'new mining village' as opposed to a colony or a satellite is that a mining 'village' is bigger and has more facilities than a colony, and it is not twinned with an existing settlement as is the case with a satellite. There are five former mining communities that come clearly into this category, four dating from the second half of the nineteenth century and one from the early twentieth century. Normanton Spring, which though small became much more complex than the colonies described in Chapter 2, emerged after the opening of Birley East Colliery in 1855. Denaby Main grew up following the opening of Denaby Main Colliery (*c.*1867) and was expanded following the sinking of Cadeby Colliery in 1893. Canklow/Brinsworth grew up in two parts to the east and west of Rotherham Main Colliery that began production in 1894. Grimethorpe was developed following the opening of Grimethorpe Colliery in 1897. And finally, Thurcroft emerged after the opening of Thurcroft Colliery in 1913. Denaby Main, Canklow/Brinsworth and Thurcroft were all on 'greenfield' sites and Normanton Spring and Grimethorpe colliery village were the successors to very small hamlets.

Normanton Spring

To the south-east of Sheffield, occupying the Shire Brook valley and beyond to the Rother valley, there is an interesting close group of settlements, now outer suburban areas of the city that grew from small hamlets or villages into substantial villages – Normanton Spring, Woodhouse and Beighton, the latter originally in Derbyshire but incorporated into the city in 1967. Normanton Spring began life as a terraced row of just five houses but by the end of the nineteenth century was a small mining village.

Records survive that show that mining was taking place in parts of the Shire Brook valley in the thirteenth century and near Beighton by the fourteenth century. In 1347 a shepherd searching for a lost sheep fell down a disused coal pit at Beighton. In the eighteenth century and the nineteenth century, a series of relatively short-lived collieries were worked in and around the Shire Brook valley including one on Birley Moor which was in production in 1733, at Base Green and High Lane from the 1820s to 1833, Wiggin Tree and Little Wiggin Tree Colliery, both of which had closed by 1913, the People's Colliery (opened in 1844), Coalbrook Colliery and Woodhouse Mill Colliery.

The first large modern colliery linked to the railway network was Birley Colliery (later Birley West Colliery), opened in 1855 at Normanton Spring, straddling the Shire Brook on the boundary between Yorkshire and Derbyshire. It was linked to the Great Central Railway via a branch mineral line. The mine was owned by the Sheffield Coal Company and at first worked the Parkgate Seam and later the Silkstone Seam. It worked until 1908. Meanwhile, the Sheffield Coal Company started to sink a new colliery in 1887, Birley East, further east along the Shire Brook valley between Woodhouse to the north and Hackenthorpe to the south. This colliery worked the Silkstone, Parkgate and Thorncliffe seams. Ownership of the colliery changed hands in 1937 when the Sheffield Coal Company was acquired by the United Steel Company Ltd. Birley East Colliery finally closed in 1943 but remained operational as a Bevin Boys Training Centre for another four years. A third modern colliery, Brookhouse, was opened by the Sheffield Coal Company north-east of Beighton in 1931. Work at the colliery was suspended for several years in the 1930s because of the poor economic conditions, but began again in 1937 when it was acquired by the United Steel Company Ltd. Four seams were worked at the colliery: Flockton, Parkgate, Thorncliffe and Silkstone. The colliery closed in 1985.

The impact of colliery development, large and small, on the Shire Brook valley and on the Rother valley beyond was immense. The landscape was transformed, the population grew dramatically and settlement expanded in every direction. Research carried out by Roy Pidcock and Christine Handley (Shire Brook Valley Heritage Group, 2007) shows graphically how the development of the two Birley collieries affected the previously tiny hamlet of Normanton Spring, which grew into a mining village. In the first part of the nineteenth century it consisted of just five cottages in Nether Wheel Row, owned by a local brickyard and quarry owner (Figure 6.1). Two of the cottages were occupied by miners and their families, the men and boys no doubt working in one of the small coal pits in the vicinity. By 1871 there were 47 cottages in the settlement and the numbers continued to grow. The fact that it was now a mining village was confirmed by the building of a school in 1871, significantly called the Birley Colliery School, funded by Thomas Dunn one of the owners of the Sheffield Coal Company. Two houses for senior colliery official were also built next to the school. The growing mining settlement also had a Wesleyan Methodist chapel that was opened in 1878 ,with seating for 150 people, and a public house, the *Normanton Spring Inn* (demolished in 2004).

An analysis of the census returns for 52 households enumerated in Normanton Spring and Normanton Hill (but excluding Coisley Hill) in 1901 shows the dramatic change in the size and make-up of the population that had occurred in less than half a century since the opening of Birley West Colliery. The enumerator noted the details of 52 households with a total population of 257, with 194 in Normanton Spring and 63 in Normanton Hill. These households contained 88 employed men and boys of whom 77 (87.5 per cent) were employed in coal mining in such varied occupations as hewer (32), filler, horse keeper, pony driver, lamp cleaner and labourer. The other occupations were stone quarry man (two), bricklayer (two), railway shunter (two) paraffin maker, publican and grocer's assistant. Only 14 of these men and boys had been born in Normanton Spring and 13 of these were the sons of migrants. Sixteen of the migrant workers

Figure 6.1 Nether Wheel Row, Normanton Spring.

had been born nearby in Gleadless, Hackenthorpe, Hollins End and Woodhouse and 13 gave their birthplace as Sheffield. But, as elsewhere, migrants had come from much further away: from the neighbouring counties of Derbyshire, Nottinghamshire and Lincolnshire from the midland counties of Leicestershire, Staffordshire and Warwickshire and there were two migrants who had been born in London, one in Barnet in Middlesex and one in Crediton in Devon. And they had come from the most obscure of places: there were three heads of household who had been born in Buckinghamshire, all of them in the tiny village of Hanslope, renowned for its lace-making. Did these Buckinghamshire migrants all move at the same time or did one move first and then inform the others of employment opportunities?

The near neighbour of Normanton Spring, Woodhouse, grew into a large village with a considerable number of miners and their families in the late nineteenth century and Beighton expanded considerably after the opening of Brookhouse Colliery in 1929.

Denaby Main

Denaby Main, the new large mining village associated with Denaby Main and Cadeby Main collieries, has gone through a number of phases of development: the creation of an 'embryonic' industrial colony in the 1860s and 1870s, limited expansion in the 1880s, further large-scale expansion in the decade following the opening of Cadeby Main Colliery in 1893 and then wholesale demolition and redevelopment since the mid-1960s.

Before 1864 and the beginning of the sinking of Denaby Main Colliery the land on which the new colliery village was to be developed was low-lying farmland to the south of the meandering River Don. The nearest villages were about a mile away: Mexborough to the west, Old Denaby to the south-west and Conisbrough to the east.

The site of Denaby Main Colliery was determined by a combination of local geology and transport considerations. At the time of its opening for commercial production in the late 1860s Denaby Main Colliery was the most easterly coal mine on the South Yorkshire Coalfield and also the deepest. It was to retain these two distinctions for more than another 30 years.

Any saving in sinking the shafts was valuable hence a site at one of the lowest points in the area on the flood plain of the River Don was inevitable. The fact that this was where the Manchester, Sheffield and Lincolnshire Railway (later Great Central Railway and then London & North Eastern Railway), navigable Don and the Don Navigation (i.e. the canal) were located was also crucial. The site chosen for the colliery consisted of fourteen acres of farmland belonging to the Fullerton estate at Thrybergh Park.

An attempt to sink a mine in Denaby township, beside the River Don, had met with failure in the 1850s because of the volume of water encountered and the expense of combating the problem. So the colliery developers who leased the land in Denaby in 1863 must have been fully aware of these problems and the expense that may be incurred. The initial capital outlay was £30,000, provided by five shareholders who by 1867 were John Buckingham Pope and Richard Pope (West Yorkshire colliery owners), Richard Pearson (also a West Yorkshire colliery owner), Edward Baines senior (a Leeds newspaper owner and Liberal MP), Joseph Crossley of Halifax (carpet manufacturer) and Joseph Huntriss (of Doncaster).

The *Doncaster Gazette* reported on 16 December 1864 that the sinking of the colliery had begun and commented on the first-class character of the machinery and said it was 'fully equal' to the task of sinking the shaft to a great depth. By August 1866 the sinkers had reached a depth of 150 yards and late in 1867 the Barnsley Seam was reached at a depth of 448 yards. This seam was nine feet eight inches thick.

By the beginning of the 1870s a small 'embryonic' colliery village had emerged next to the colliery (Figure 6.2). In his book, *From Doncaster to Hallamshire*, published in 1879, John Tomlinson wrote a detailed description of this early village:

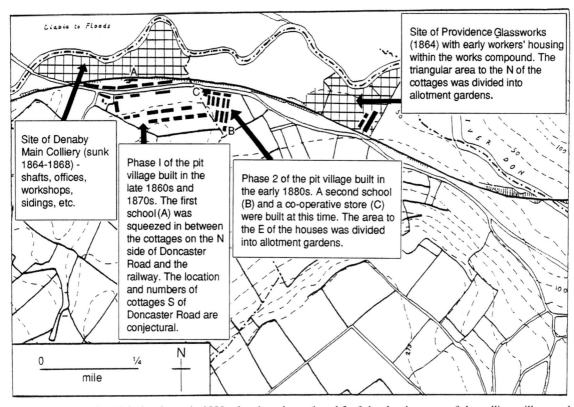

Site of Providence Glassworks (1864) with early workers' housing within the works compound. The triangular area to the N of the cottages was divided into allotment gardens.

Site of Denaby Main Colliery (sunk 1864-1868) - shafts, offices, workshops, sidings, etc.

Phase I of the pit village built in the late 1860s and 1870s. The first school (A) was squeezed in between the cottages on the N side of Doncaster Road and the railway. The location and numbers of cottages S of Doncaster Road are conjectural.

Phase 2 of the pit village built in the early 1880s. A second school (B) and a co-operative store (C) were built at this time. The area to the E of the houses was divided into allotment gardens.

Liable to Floods

0   ¼

mile

N

Figure 6.2 Denaby Main by the early 1880s showing phases 1 and 2 of the development of the colliery village and Kilner's Glassworks and associated housing.

... Not very long ago the 'pit-hollow presented a few unsightly excrescences, or spoil banks, with an engine house, rough 'head-gear' and a number of small one-storied dwellings not inaptly termed 'sparrow-barracks'.

...the aspect and associations of Denaby have greatly changed ... Here, right in one's path, looms a gigantic colliery with its tall chimneys, elevated head-gear, huge spoil-banks, tramways, workshops, offices and long rows of cottages – a thickly populated village, all in a lump.

... I noticed a little school-room in a hollow place, under the shadow of that pit-hill – a not very eligible site, although young lungs breathe freely. I observed also a dissenting Chapel and a plain, unromantic church, half-warehouse and half cottage, with a very wooden porch and arched belfry, in the latest Gothic style (Tomlinson, 149–50).

Tomlinson's Sparrow Barracks were over Grey's Bridge, half a mile to the west of the colliery in Mexborough, opposite the *Miners' Arms*. The rest of the early village (Tomlinson's 'long rows of cottages') seems to have consisted of cottages, more than 80 in all, standing adjacent to the colliery along the northern side of Doncaster Road. It is also likely that a substantial number of the cottages on the south side of Doncaster Road, on the south side of Amberley Street and the north side of Cliff View, date from this period of development. The OS Six-Inch map of 1903 shows a school in the backyard of the cottages on the north side of Doncaster Road, presumably the one referred to by Tomlinson. There was also a bye-law application for a Wesleyan chapel at Denaby Main in 1870. At this stage both the colliery and the colliery village were in Denaby township in Mexborough parish near the boundary with Conisbrough parish.

In 1864, while the colliery was being sunk, another development was taking place. In that year a glassworks, the Providence Glassworks, was opened at Denaby Main by Kilner Brothers of Thornhill Lees, Dewsbury, manufacturers of the famous 'Kilner jar'. The glassworks and its associated residential colony of the glassworks employees and their families were located over half a mile to the east of Denaby Main Colliery on low land to the north of the Doncaster Road in Conisbrough parish. In 1879 about 200 men, women and boys were employed there, many of them in what Tomlinson described as 'two rows of comfortable cottages, numbering upwards of 40 in all, attached to the works'.

That was the end of the first phase of development. But in 1881 a second phase began when the colliery company leased six acres in Underhill Field in Conisbrough parish from Andrew Montagu of Melton Hall. On this land they laid out Rossington Street, Tickhill Street, Melton Street and Melton View and built about 100 new houses. They also built part of the Co-operative stores in Melton View and a second school on Tickhill Street.

The third phase of development began in 1889, when the colliery company made an agreement with Dame Georgina Copley of Sprotborough for the exploitation of the Barnsley Seam beneath Dame Georgina's Sprotbrorough, Cadeby, Scawsby and Marr Grange estates under the Magnesian Limestone outcrop, which overlooked Denaby Main to the east. This would be the first incursion in South Yorkshire into the concealed coalfield. In 1889 the *Doncaster Gazette* was able to report that work on the new colliery – Cadeby Main Colliery – had begun. It opened in 1893.

In anticipation of the expansion of their mining operations, the colliery company set about acquiring more land on which to extend their colliery village and this ushered in a decade of substantial settlement expansion (Figure 6.3). In December 1889 they leased more land in Underhill Field from Andrew Montagu of Melton Hall and bye-law applications to build houses were submitted in 1891 and 1893. This resulted in the development of Marr Street, Sprotbrough Street, Edlington Street, Clifton Street and Firbeck Street. Altogether 348 dwellings were erected together with three shops in Wood View on Doncaster Road. To match this residential development another school was built at the top of Rossington Street (opened in 1893).

Even further expansion was foreshadowed in 1893 when a further ten acres were leased from Andrew Montagu immediately to the east of the plot leased in 1889. The colliery company then proceeded to lay out and build six more streets: Balby, Blythe, Loversall, Scawsby, Cusworth and Wadworth. Altogether they built 307 four-roomed houses and 96 six-roomed houses on this plot.

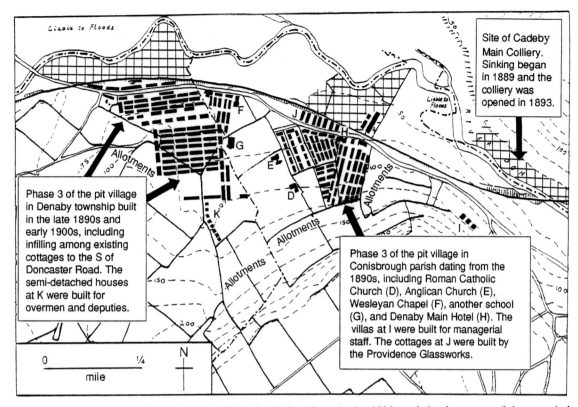

Figure 6.3 Further extension (phase 3) to Denaby Main village in the 1890s and the first years of the twentieth century.

They also built a public house – *Denaby Main Hotel* (or 'The Drum' as it was more popularly known). A little later (1897) a bye-law application was made to build St Alban's Roman Catholic Church which was completed in 1898.

During this phase of development of the colliery village, Kilner Brothers made plans to enlarge the housing provision for their workers. An application was made in 1892 to build 150 houses on the narrow strip of land south of their works between the then Sheffield, Manchester and Lincolnshire Railway and Doncaster Road. They eventually built 60 houses on four short streets – named John, William, George and Thornhill, running at right angles to the road and the railway.

The turn of the century saw another surge of building which was to more or less round off the development of the colliery village. This was in Denaby township, the scene of the earliest village development thirty years earlier. A bye-law application was made in March 1898 to build 233 houses in Adwick Street, Annerley Street, Barnbrough Street and Doncaster Road among pre-existing housing. Another application was made in November 1901 to build a further 552 houses on Annerley Street. Cliff View, Warmsworth Street, Braithwell Street, Maltby Street, Ravensfield Street, Bolton Street and Tickhill Street. Land was conveyed to the colliery company for these two developments in March 1899. Separate bye-law applications were made for smaller adjoining developments in Tickhill Street (31 houses) and Tickhill Square (16 houses). The houses in Tickhill Square were semi-detached, with front and back gardens and WCs. They were allocated to pit deputies and overmen.

At this time two other developments took place at the other (eastern) end of the village. All Saints' Church was built in 1900 and six superior semi-detached villas – Hayden House, Dunragit House, Rockland House, Ashlea House, Goodnestone House and Albany House were built in Buckingham Road for managerial and other professional company staff (see Figure 1.6).

By the beginning of the twentieth century Denaby Main colliery village was virtually complete and provided accommodation for about 2,500 employees at the two collieries. The morphology of the village was relatively simple. To the north of the main railway line lay Denaby Main Colliery, Cadeby Main Colliery and their spoil heaps and a complex network of mineral railways and sidings. This also included Kilners' Glassworks and some of their early housing. To the south of the main railway and predominantly south of Doncaster Road lay Denaby Main village containing about 1,500 houses. The housing was in two large blocks, one in Denaby township, the other in Conisbrough. Between the two main blocks of residential development lay a wedge of non-residential land containing schools, an Anglican church, a Roman Catholic church, a cricket ground and a football ground. By 1930 this area also contained the Fullerton Hospital, the Miners' Welfare Institute, a cemetery and, at the Doncaster Road end a park, market place and a cinema. Doncaster Road contained both housing and a ribbon of commercial development. Lastly, surrounding the village in the west, south and east were extensive allotment gardens. By 1900, although the toilets were still earth closets (middens), facilities in the miners' homes had improved in two respects: gas lighting had replaced candles and paraffin lamps and a reservoir had been built on the North Cliff to the south of the village which was filled with water pumped from Cadeby Main Colliery and then supplied to the village by standpipes.

One of the main characteristics of the 'completed' mining village was the uniformity of it all. Each street was straight, and within each block of development the streets were laid out in parallel rows of red brick houses separated in large parts of the village by wide communal yards with blocks of brick-built outside lavatories. Even the pavements were of red brick. This uniformity was carried through in the most minute detail: almost all the buildings erected in the fifteen years from about 1890 – colliers' houses, the villas built for senior staff and the colliery offices – were characterized by a horizontal decorative brick band in the wall and by a triangular tile decoration along the roof ridge. The absence of trees and shrubs in almost all the residential parts of the village emphasised the unrelieved uniformity of the place. This uniformity was even carried through into the street names which with just a few exceptions were named after local villages.

It is interesting to record three very contrasting evaluations of the village by people writing about it in the period between the beginning of the twentieth century and the 1930s. Mr Eldon

Bankes, KC, speaking on behalf of Denaby and Cadeby Collieries in 1904 at a hearing held in connection with the 'bag-muck strike' of 1902–03 when striking miners and their families were ejected from their homes, said:

> *At the time when the strike occurred they* [the colliery company] *owned I think some 1,400 houses, They were congregated together close to the Denaby Pit, and they formed the village of Denaby Main. The company had all along taken the greatest pains and succeeded in their efforts in making these houses as sanitary and as comfortable as possible; and, in addition, they had taken great pains to introduce into that village anything that occurred to them to be for the welfare of the men in the way of reading rooms, and recreation rooms and matters of that kind; and I do not think it can be disputed that the village as owned and managed by this Company was in itself what might be called something equivalent to a model mining village.*

In complete contrast, a reporter writing in the *Christian Budget* five years earlier on 8 November 1899 under the heading 'THE WORST VILLAGE IN ENGLAND' said

> *I am sitting down to write this article in numb despair, for the mining community I have to describe is so repulsive that many who have never been near it will refuse to credit the story* (quoted by MacFarlane, 1978, p.180).

Writing in 1934, Roger Dataller, ex-miner and Oxford graduate, and at the time working for the WEA in South Yorkshire, was equally critical of the very earliest housing tucked in between the colliery and Doncaster Road:

> *The oldest houses in D_____ (and it is only fair to announce that they are the oldest) have been built, so to speak, in the backyard of the colliery itself: rows of grim boxes identical in size, and conceived, one feels, in the mind of some satanic toymaker. It is only a step from each kitchen to each W.C. The bare yards are unpaved – a pother of dust in the dry weather, a quagmire in wet. The colliery loco shunts beyond the boundary wall, and the pervading presence of the superstructure can be evaded in these houses only by a universal lowering of blinds. I find it impossible to think of D_____ without an inordinate impulse to seize upon the architect of this monstrosity and haul him by the nose through the horror of his creation.* (Dataller, 1934, p.13).

Conditions must indeed have been squalid in the oldest, smallest and most crowded parts of the village. In these areas there were no private gardens or yards and toilet facilities and water supplies were shared. In the absence of public or private transport, the proximity of the village to the collieries could not be avoided. At least the prevailing wind blew smoke and dust away from the village. And some of the housing built for overmen and deputies in Wheatley Street,

Tickhill Street and Tickhill Square were very sound and survive to this day. And in their prime the villas in Buckingham Road would not have been out of place in the most affluent Victorian and Edwardian suburbs anywhere in the country.

But whether the houses of the colliery village were soundly built or not or well appointed or not, was secondary to the fact that they were owned by the colliery company. As the social historian Jim MacFarlane has pointed out (MacFarlane, 1972, 1987) in his work on the village, this meant that the loss of accommodation became as much of an issue as the loss of wages whenever there was a dispute or whenever a miner was dismissed for whatever reason. There were very few locals among the original 'colonists' in Denaby Main village, and so there were no well developed local traditions and allegiances. And like the working men in the collieries there, the colliery proprietors of Denaby Main were not local; they were determined, experienced, risk-taking entrepreneurs, largely from West Yorkshire. They were determined to make their venture work – and on their own terms. These unique circumstances meant that everyone employed by the company tended to fall into one of two camps – they were either union men or company men. The result of this situation was that every time there was a major dispute between the miners' union and the colliery company, the families of the men involved living in company housing were made homeless. This happened in 1869, 1877, 1885 and 1902–03. Moreover, as the nineteenth century progressed the village became larger and larger and more employees at the two collieries were housed in company property. During disputes, large parts of the village had to be evacuated and the population dispersed to be temporarily housed in churches and chapels in the surrounding area, in the houses of family and friends not in company property and even in tents in the surrounding countryside, only to return in most cases (and only on one occasion, in 1869, in triumph) to the village – but not necessarily to the same house – once the dispute was resolved. The village, therefore, was not only a convenient place of residence for the mining population, but also a means of social control for the mining company during the years of heaviest investment during the last four decades of the nineteenth century.

The latest phase of development began in the mid-1960s. It was decided that the village, the oldest parts of which were almost 100 years old, was obsolete, and a redevelopment plan was embarked upon which took two decades to complete. This saw Denaby Main rise from the dust as a modern community with the most up-to-date housing and community facilities based on the latest planning principles and ideas of housing design. Ironically by the time the redevelopment of the village was complete, it was no longer a mining village. Denaby Main Colliery closed in 1968 and Cadeby Main in 1986.

Relatively little of the physical fabric of the original mining village remains. The entrance to the site of Denaby Main Colliery is marked by a colliery winding wheel and much of the surface operational area of Cadeby Main Colliery was developed as the short-lived Earth Centre. Much of the rest of the sites of the two collieries had been landscaped by the end of the twentieth century. By that time, in the village itself, the Roman Catholic church still stood as an imposing landmark, but the large school built in the 1890s stood empty. And the large Wesleyan chapel, and the later cinema, although still standing were used then as a body building and fitness centre and photographic laboratory respectively. A few streets of houses built in the 1890s also survive among the modern housing. On Wheatley Street and Tickhill Street there are substantial terrace houses and in Tickhill Square semi-detached houses, their origins betrayed by the tell-tale decorative band of brickwork.

Canklow

I have called this settlement Canklow because the colliery with which it was associated and part of the new colliery settlement lay at foot of a long slope clothed by the 243-acre Canklow Wood, leading down to the River Rother. But the River Rother formed a township boundary and the new colliery settlement that had emerged by the beginning of the twentieth century was in two ancient townships of the ancient parish of Rotherham: Whiston to the east of the Rother and Brinsworth to the west of the River Rother.

The reason for the growth of a colliery settlement was the sinking of Rotherham Main Colliery, which began in 1890 on the Brinsworth side of the River Rother, beside the Midland Railway. The colliery owners were John Brown & Company Limited, the Sheffield steel manufacturers of the Atlas Works in the Lower Don valley. The first coal was raised in 1894 and John Brown & Co Ltd remained owners until nationalisation. The colliery closed in 1954. Over its lifetime five coal seams were worked: High Hazels, Barnsley, Swallow Wood, Parkgate and Silkstone. The coke ovens at the colliery produced coke for the firm's steelworks.

Before the sinking of Rotherham Main the only buildings that existed were Canklow Bridge over the River Rother and Canklow corn mill with its mill dam. But by the beginning of the twentieth century, housing for the workers had been erected on both sides of the River Rother. At the foot of Canklow Wood a long line cottages made up of eight terraces, each containing ten residences, stretched towards the centre of the town along Canklow Lane. At the southern end of this line of cottages stood a school.

Three hundred yards further south, again on the edge of Canklow Wood was Canklow Terrace, made up of three short terraces each containing six residences, this time for senior colliery officials. These terraces survive to this day. In 1901 Canklow Terrace had a population of 148 with an average of eight people in every household. Of these inhabitants, 47 of the 48 employed men and boys worked at the colliery. Eleven of these were deputies and many of the others had specialized trades such as winding repair man, head lamp keeper, colliery blacksmith, electrical engineer and so on. Most of these colliery employees (70 per cent) had been born in South Yorkshire and all the others were from the West Midlands (places in Shropshire, Staffordshire, Warwickshire and Worcestershire) or from elsewhere in the Midlands (Derbyshire and Leicestershire).

On the Brinsworth side of the river the colliery settlement grew up as one very long street, called after the name of the steel works of the owners, Atlas Street (Figure 6.4). It was a perfectly

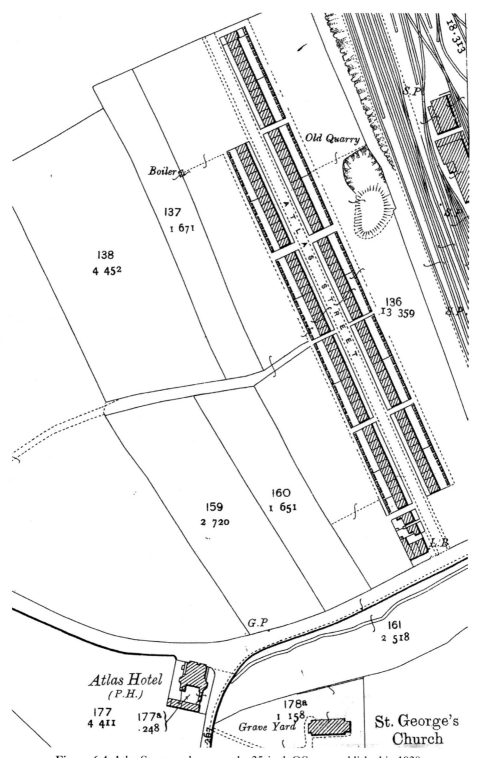

Figure 6.4 Atlas Street as shown on the 25-inch OS map published in 1928.

straight street village. Apart from the co-operative stores, every building was residential. Beyond the southern end of the street on the road to Tinsley stood the *Atlas Hotel* and St George's church. Altogether 747 men, women and children lived on Atlas Street in 1901. In that year there were 242 employed men and boys living on the street, of whom 212 (87.6 per cent) were colliery workers. Among the other workers there was a night soil man and a stick hawker. And most of these men and boys were migrants. Only 40 (16.5 per cent) were born within what is now the modern metropolitan borough of Rotherham. Forty-one (17 per cent) were from the rest of South Yorkshire and another 24 (9.9 per cent) were from other parts of Yorkshire. Other important sources of migrant workers were Derbyshire, Leicestershire, Staffordshire and Shropshire. Among surprising birthplaces of residents of Atlas Street were Maidstone in Kent, Dunstable in Hertfordshire and Saxmundham in Suffolk. And as usual there were a few miners from Wales, Scotland and Ireland.

Two households in Atlas Street exemplify the fact that South Yorkshire's mining villages were teeming with migrant families. John Compton was a hewer born in West Bromwich in the 'Black Country' of Staffordshire and his wife was from Donnington in Shropshire, and probably a migrant to the Black Country. Their eldest two children, daughter Phyllis (15) and son Percy (13) were born in Hednesford in Staffordshire, but their two youngest children (aged seven and three) had been born in Hucknall and Bulwell in Nottinghamshire. The family were obviously very recent migrants to South Yorkshire. Living with them were two boarders, both hewers, one from Wakefield and the other from Shropshire. Another family, the Smiths, had moved long distances across the country. William Smith was a colliery blacksmith born in Saxmundham in Suffolk. He had obviously moved north at an early age and married his wife Eliza who had been born in Swadlicote in Derbyshire. The family had obviously then moved north to South Yorkshire where three children, aged 19, 17 and 15 in 1901, had been born (in Rotherham). They had then moved to north-east England. Their son John, aged ten, had been born in Gateshead in County Durham and a six year-old daughter, Mary, had been born in Backworth in Northumberland. Then they had moved south again to South Yorkshire where their youngest child Florence, aged four, had been born – in Canklow.

Grimethorpe

Those who have only heard of the place as a mining settlement could well believe that the name Grimethorpe (or Grimey as it is known locally), is a Victorian invention like Dickens' Coketown in *Hard Times*. But nothing could be further from the truth. Grimethorpe was first recorded in the thirteenth century as *Grimestorp* and was obviously an old name at that time, being derived from *Grimr*, an Old Norse personal name and *torp*, a Danish Viking place-name element meaning an outlying farm or hamlet, hence 'Grim's outlying farm or hamlet. In the Middle Ages it lay on the edge of Brierley deer park, with its moated manor house set within the park, the site of which still survives and is marked as Hall Steads to the north-east of Grimethorpe.

In 1831 Joseph Hunter in his *South Yorkshire* described Grimethorpe as 'a few dwellings near an ancient mill'. And nothing much had changed by the time of the sinking of Grimethorpe Colliery in 1894. The Six-inch Ordnance Survey map surveyed in 1890 and published in 1894 shows that it was still a small hamlet clustered around Grimethorpe Green. The land on which the hamlet had grown up and the surrounding farmland on which development was about to take place were both part of the estate of F. J. S. Foljambe Esquire of Osberton Hall in Nottinghamshire. There was a manor house, two farms (Manor Farm and Foldhead Farm) and a few cottages including the Mill Cottages. There was a small school (erected 1868), a primitive methodist chapel (erected 1869), but no public house. The population was only 87 in 1891. Although there were nine mine workers living in Grimethorpe in 1891, most of those in employment worked in rural occupations such as farmer, farm foreman, farm servant, farm labourer, groom and woodman.

But all this was to change dramatically. At 1.30 pm, on Monday 8 October 1894, the directors of Mitchell Main Colliery Company held a 'Turning of the First Sod' ceremony for the new Grimethorpe Colliery. And what a ceremony! Many of the guests were conveyed from Cudworth railway station in saloon and First Class railway carriages along a specially constructed branch line to the colliery site. The party of guests then listened to speeches while gathered around two white circles painted on the ground marking the places where the colliery's two shafts were to be sunk. In the centre of each circle was a white post with a flag flying. Mr Joseph Mitchell of Bolton Hall, the company's managing director, said that the Barnsley Seam would be expected to be reached at 500 yards in about two years and that the new coalfield to be exploited extended to 3,000 acres. He said he expected the new colliery to be capable of producing 2,500 tons of coal a day, three-quarters of a million tons a year. Another of the speakers, Mr C. J. Tyas, acknowledged that they were industrializing a rural area when he said that the company had taken the best part of the Badsworth hunt country and that the runs some of those there had enjoyed for so long would soon be impossible. After the turning of the first sod ceremony, guests enjoyed a hearty lunch, the menu consisting of roast sirloin of beef, braised beef, pigeon pie, ham and tongue, boiled and roast chicken, turkey, grouse and pheasant, accompanied by cheese, celery and salads, followed by a selection of desserts. All this was washed down with a selection of champagne, sherry, claret and hock. And to round off the occasion, cigars, cognac and Scotch whisky were provided!

In 1896 the ownership of the colliery was transferred from the Mitchell Main Colliery Company to the Carlton Main Colliery Company. The seven-feet-thick Barnsley Seam, in great demand as a steam coal, was reached in 1897 at a depth of 560 yards in two shafts and production began in the same year. In 1925 the workings were deepened to the almost equally thick Parkgate Seam, an excellent coking coal, at 839 yards. Meanwhile in 1915, Ferrymoor Colliery was sunk immediately to the west of Grimethorpe Colliery by Hodroyd Colliery Company to work the Shafton Seam at a depth of 56 yards. In 1919 Ferrymoor Colliery was also acquired by the Carlton Main Colliery Company.

The prediction by the reporter of the *Barnsley Chronicle* at the turning of the first sod ceremony came true very quickly. In the 13 October edition of the newspaper, he stated that 'Instances are common enough hereabouts of sleepy, out-of-the-way villages being suddenly transformed into busy centres of population through the sinking of a new mine. Such a change, there is every reason to believe, will shortly be experienced in the village of Grimethorpe.' By 1911 the population had risen to 3,262 and by 1931 had reached 5,208. And in the early years of its growth, the population of the new colliery village were all migrants. They had come not only short distances from neighbouring mining and farming villages and from the industrial town of Barnsley, less than five miles to the west (itself a scene of major nineteenth century population growth with a population of 50,000 in 1911 an increase of 32,000 since 1861), but from far and wide.

In the 1901 census of population, some four years after the first coal had been raised at Grimethorpe Colliery, the original hamlet of Grimethorpe and the new mining village were still

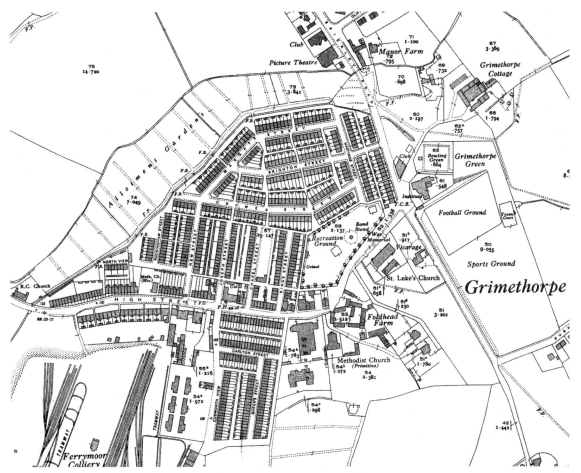

Figure 6.5 The central part of Grimethorpe with the early terraced rows built for miners and their families as shown on the 25-inch OS map published in 1929.

two separate entities, being described by the census enumerator as 'The Hamlet of Grimethorpe together with all the new cottages at Grimethorpe Colliery'. So new was the mining village in 1901 that three of the six streets of cottages were simply called 'One Street', 'Two Street' and 'Three Street' (Figure 6.5). One of the three streets that was properly named was Joseph Street, the central one of the five running immediately north from High Street. Living in Joseph Street in 1901 were migrants not only from all parts of Yorkshire, but also from all the neighbouring counties of Lancashire, Cheshire, Derbyshire, Nottinghamshire and Lincolnshire and from the midland counties of Leicestershire, Shropshire, Staffordshire and Worcestershire. There were also migrants in Grimethorpe in 1901 from Bedfordshire, Durham, Gloucestershire, Wales and Ireland and there was even a Cockney who had been born in London's East End at Bromley-By-Bow.

Not surprisingly, Grimethorpe grew out of all recognition in the three decades between the opening of the colliery in 1897 and the late 1920s. The settlement had expanded in all directions. By 1929 the two collieries, with their headgear, engine houses, mineral railways and sidings, reservoirs, sludge ponds, spoil heaps and brick works covered an area more than four times as big as the original hamlet. Areas of brick housing to accommodate the migrant families to the area had developed, swamping the farm buildings and cottages of the original inhabitants.

As early as 1904, as shown on the Ordnance Survey 25 inches to one mile map, a substantial mining village had been laid out between Grimethorpe Colliery and the original hamlet of Grimethorpe. Although none of the streets were named on the 1904 map, the compact mining village then consisted of what became High Street with Joseph Street, Chapel Street and King's Street to the north and Carlton Street, Queen's Street, and Cudworth View to the south. Standing separate from the village in 1904, at the western end of High Street, stood the Wesleyan Methodist chapel, by 1929 engulfed by the expansion of the village in that direction. The other major buildings in the village by 1904 were the mainly red brick St Luke's parish church which had been opened by the Archbishop of York in March of that year, and Grimethorpe School at the eastern end of High Street, next to Foldhead Farm, which in 1904 had 375 pupils. This school was built in addition to the small school, which had been built in 1868 and which stood across the road from St Luke's church. It had been demolished by the time the 1929 sheet was published.

By 1929 the area covered by housing in Grimethorpe was four times as big as it was in 1904. Most of the growth was to the north of the original mining village, with more terrace housing on the streets named after seaside resorts – Brighton, Cromer, Hastings, Margate – and in the semi-detached houses on Brierley Road, Willow Dene Road, Park Road and Clifton Road. Another large development of semi-detached housing on winding roads and with large private gardens had also been built next to Lady Wood, in contrast to the closely packed grid-iron layout of the earliest housing.

By the end of the 1920s Grimethorpe had all the attributes of a self-contained community. The High Street was full of shops including the 52nd branch of the Barnsley British Co-operative Society, grocers, greengrocers, butchers, drapers, hairdressers, a confectioner, a chemist's shop, a dentist's surgery, two fish and chip shops and two wireless dealers. It had churches (including a Roman Catholic church) and chapels, schools, a public house (the *Grimethorpe Hotel*), a colliery institute, a working men's club, a British Legion club, a cinema, a recreation ground with a bandstand, a miners' welfare recreation ground, a bowling green, a football ground, a cemetery, extensive allotment gardens and, of course, the world-famous Grimethorpe Colliery Band, founded in 1917.

Thurcroft

Thurcroft lies right on the eastern edge of the exposed coalfield. Despite its name which is part Old Norse and part Old English and means 'Thori's enclosure', Thurcroft did not exist as a village until the twentieth century. Before then it consisted of Thurcroft Hall in its park and a small number of farms; no church, no chapel, no school. As the Reverend Joseph Hunter put it in his *South Yorkshire* (1828–31, p. 294), 'Thurcroft Hall is a handsome mansion with a view of great extent of open country'. The hall and the surrounding estate, which had previously been owned by the Mirfin and Beckwith families, was bought in the nineteenth century by a Sheffield brewer, Thomas Marrian. In the 1901 census it is recorded that his son, also called Thomas, was living at the Hall with his wife Fanny, his sister and five servants (including a butler). Thomas Marrian Junior leased the mineral rights to the Rothervale Colliery Company in 1902. The area was served by two railways, the LMS and the LNER.

Sinking of the colliery began in 1909 and the Barnsley Seam was reached in 1913 at 850 yards deep. The Rothervale Colliery Company was taken over by the United Steel Company in 1921 who then built brickworks and coke ovens at the colliery. By the 1930s more than 2,000 men were employed at the colliery. Working of the Barnsley Seam ceased in 1968. Other deeper seams worked at the colliery were Swallow Wood, Haigh Moor and Parkgate. The colliery closed in 1991 when it employed 600 men. But then a group of former employees put in a bid to buy out the colliery and keep it in production, but this venture failed and it was not re-opened.

In 1901 before the colliery was sunk, the Thurcroft area was part of the parish of Laughton, with a parish population of 631. But the area on which the colliery and the colliery village was to be built was farmland belonging to three farms – New Orchard Farm, Sawn Moor Farm and Green Arbour Farm with a population of just 20. At New Orchard Farm lived the farmer (a widow, her son and his daughter and a horseman); at Sawn Moor Farm lived a farmer, two domestic servants and a horseman; in Sawn Moor Farm Cottage lived the farm foreman, his wife, five children and his mother-in-law, and at Green Arbour Farm lived the farmer (a widow) and a horseman. This rural area and the way of life of its inhabitants would in the next decade be totally transformed. In 1921, just eight years after the colliery opened, the population of the parish had risen to 2,679, most of it associated with the growth of the new colliery village at Thurcroft.

The colliery was located to the east of New Orchard Farm and it was planned to build housing for the miners immediately to the south, south of Woodhouse Green and Sandy Lane on either side of Green Arbour Road. The first streets were laid out and built by the colliery company in 1914, composed of short rows of terraced housing. These were John Street, Charles Street and Peter Street (Figure 6.6), at right angles to Woodhouse Green to the west of Green Arbour Road and West Street, Church Street, South Street and Katherine Street to the south of Sandy Lane and to the east of Green Arbour Road. These cottages were influenced by the 'model village' concept that was being used in the construction of other new mining villages on the concealed coalfield at this time, for example, at Maltby and Woodlands. Each house had its own front garden and inside there was a bath connected to a copper to provide a direct supply of hot water. A few years later villas were built on New Orchard Lane for the manager and other senior colliery officials and their families. Further residential development by the colliery company took place in the mid-1920s to the east of the pre-First World War village on Steadfolds Lane, Laughton Road, The Crescent and Crescent End in what became known locally as the Wembley area, it

Figure 6.6 Peter Street, Thurcroft in 2016.

being constructed at the same time as Wembley Stadium in London. The 1930s saw further residential development, this time by Rotherham Rural District Council on Sawn Moor Avenue, Waverley Avenue, Morthen Villas and Green Arbour Road and in the 1950s the large Ivanhoe estate was laid out, again by Rotherham RDC in the south-west, in which the streets were named after characters and places in Sir Walter Scott's novel. The village now has a population of more than 5,000.

The provision of basic services in permanent long-lasting buildings lagged behind the provision of housing. A temporary corrugated iron Anglican church was erected in 1914 and about the same time a wooden Wesleyan Methodist church was built, together with a temporary school building, and even the Co-operative store and the doctor's surgery were in wooden huts in the early days. A permanent school building for junior girls and boys was eventually completed in 1925, but the foundation stone for the St Simon and St Jude stone Anglican church was not laid until 1937.

Chapter 7

Mining Settlements on the Concealed Coalfield

These are perhaps the most distinctive type of colliery settlement that can be recognised in South Yorkshire. There are far fewer former colliery settlements on the concealed coalfield than on the exposed coalfield to the west. Altogether there are ten, of which four lie in the western Magnesian Limestone belt (Maltby, New Edlington, Woodlands, Skellow/ Carcroft), four in the central Bunter Pebble Beds belt (Armthorpe, New Bentley, New Rossington and Askern/Instoneville) and two on the Humberhead Levels (Hatfield and Moorends at Thorne) in the extreme eastern part of South Yorkshire. This type of colliery village or small town is characterised by its twentieth century origin (the ten collieries began production between 1907 and 1924), its large size, and, in most cases, by its planned layout and the influence of the garden city movement on the well laid-out estates of geometrical design. The exceptions to the last two characteristics are Bentley New Village, Carcroft and New Edlington, which contain early housing layouts much more like the grid-iron terraced villages of the eastern half of the exposed coalfield.

The new mining settlements on the concealed coalfield were often laid out next to existing agricultural villages like the satellite settlements on the exposed coalfield and sometimes have 'New' in their names to distinguish them from their ancient agricultural neighbours as in New Edlington next to Old Edlington, New Rossington next to Rossington and Bentley New Village next to Bentley. One of the new villages, Instoneville, carries the name of the colliery chairman, Samuel Instone, having previously been called Askern Model Village or by its new residents simpy as New Village. Askern also has the distinction that the existing settlement that had grown up before the opening of the colliery, was not an agricultural village or, as in the case of Thorne, a small market town, but a spa resort. Kelly's *Directory of the West Riding of Yorkshire* in 1912 reported that the medicinal springs at Askern were noted for the cure of rheumatism, gout, sciatica and scorbutic diseases. By 1932 Roger Dataller, then working for the WEA, wrote that 'the dark hand of industry had muddied the waters'. He went on to note that one of the bath houses had become 'a furniture emporium, the traditional name being still in position across the façade', and the miners' welfare was an adapted hydro 'coveniently elevated and standing in its own grounds' (Dataller, 1934, pp. 107-109).

All these settlements housed miners at widely spaced collieries, so another characteristic of these planned settlements is that they are separated from each other by large tracts of countryside, unlike the colliery settlements of the exposed coalfield which often merge into each other as in the Dearne valley between Wombwell and Denaby Main. For example, a stranger in the past, approaching New Rossington from Tickhill along Stripe Road (B6463) and passing through farmed countryside with isolated residences called Dumpling Castle Farm, Hesley Lodge and Jasmine Cottage, would be completely surprised to suddenly come into a large bustling mining settlement.

Four detailed case studies are included: Woodlands which was established after Brodsworth Main Colliery came into production in 1907, the new model village at Maltby that started to be built in 1910 to house miners and their families who worked at Maltby Main Colliery that began to produce coal in 1911; New Edlington that was built to house the miners of Yorkshire Main Colliery that opened in 1913 and New Rossington which housed miners working at Rossington Main Colliery which began production in 1916.

Woodlands

The large colliery settlement of Woodlands (which includes Woodlands Model village, Highfields, Woodlands East, Woodlands Central and Woodlands New Estate) was designed and built to house the families of miners who worked at Brodsworth Main Colliery, four miles north-west of Doncaster beside the Great North Road (A638) and near the existing villages of Brodsworth and Pickburn to the east and Adwick-le-Street to the west. The colliery exploited the coal below the country estate of the Thellusson family who lived at Brodsworth Hall, immediately to the south of Brodsworth, a large house built in the Italianate style between 1861–63 and surrounded by beautiful gardens and parkland. The colliery site was served by three railways: the Great Central, the Great Northern and the Hull & Barnsley Railway. The original mining company was a partnership between the Hickleton Main Colliery Company and the Staveley Coal & Iron Company. Arthur Markham MP, one of the directors of the Hickleton Main Company, became its first chairman. The first sod was cut on 23 October 1905 by Mr Charles Thellusson and his wife using what had by now become the traditional silver spade and decorated small wheelbarrow (on display for visitors to inspect at Brodsworth Hall, acquired by English Heritage in 1990). Two shafts were sunk to the Barnsley Seam at a depth of 595 yards and production of coal began in 1907. At the same time a brickworks was built near Pickburn that could produce 30,000 bricks a day to supply bricks for the colliery buildings and the proposed new colliery village. The colliery was a large-scale enterprise, indeed the largest colliery in South Yorkshire, employing 2,400 men as early as 1912, and it was claimed in the 1920s that more coal was drawn every day and every week than from any other colliery in the world! In 1937 it became part of Doncaster Amalgamated Collieries (which also included Bullcroft, Firbeck, Hicklteon Main, Markham Main and Yorkshire Main collieries) and remained part of that group until nationalisation in 1947. It remained one of the country's biggest and most productive collieries in the post-war period, and in the late 1950s employed 3,600 men. In 1970 the colliery was linked underground with Bullcroft Colliery and coal from Bullcroft was raised at Brodsworth.

At the end of the 1980s it still employed 1,500 men. Altogether four seams were worked at the pit: Barnsley, Dunsil, Parkgate and Thorncliffe. The colliery closed in 1990. The colliery site including the pit heaps has now been landscaped and forms Brodsworth Community Woodland, covering 99 hectares of broadleaf woodland, meadow and valley wetland.

Being some distance from other large settlements and requiring a sizeable skilled workforce, the need for a nearby purpose-built colliery settlement was paramount from the very beginning. For this reason, from 1907, the new 'model' colliery village of Woodlands started to emerge in the parkland and countryside surrounding a country house called *Woodlands* bought from the Thellussons that lay directly to the east of the colliery (the house itself was converted into a Miners' Institute). Determined to build a high quality settlement based on garden city principles, Arthur Markham enlisted the help of Percy Houlton, who had designed New Bolsover and Creswell model villages on the Derbyshire coalfield, to oversee the design of the new village. Creswell was constructed around an oval-shaped green and New Bolsover on three sides of a tree-lined rectangular-shaped green. So, it is not surprising that the first area to be developed

Figure 7.1 Houses around The Park in Woodlands in 2016.

in 1907, The Park, consisted of 120 cottages set around an area of parkland containing trees (Figure 7.1). The cottages are in various designs with an indoor toilet, and inside and out must have seemed revolutionary both to new residents and visitors alike (which included King George V and Queen Mary in 1912). An extension to the original development, called The Field, dating from 1908, lay to the north of The Park, separated from it by an area containing community buildings including All Saints church dedicated in 1913, the building costs having been provided by Charles Thellusson, a Wesleyan methodist chapel, a primitive methodist chapel, two schools and a branch of the Doncaster Co-operative Society. This extension contained more than 500 houses in a design consisting of an outer road called The Crescent in an elliptical shape with spokes (West Avenue, East Avenue, Central Avenue, Green Lane, Quarry Lane, Harold Avenue and Marson Avenue (the latter named after Benjamin Marson, who was in charge of building operations). Street trees were planted along the main thoroughfares. A further 30 properties were built in 1909 for senior colliery officials.

As the colliery developed and employment numbers rose a second model village was designed and built, again under the supervision of Benjamin Marson. This was Highfields, south of Woodlands, begun in 1911. Here, more than 300 houses were built on a roughly rectangular site with two long roads, Coppice Road and South Street, running west to east, a few houses facing the Great North road in the east, and at the western end Market Street with houses on one side and shops on the other. Behind Market Street a school, a mission church and a miners' institute were built. The houses were built in short terraced rows. A second phase of the Highfields development was completed after the end of the First World War between Market Street and the Roman Road to the west containing about 150 houses. In 1916 the relative isolation of the new mining village was ended when it was connected to Doncaster by tram, with a terminus at the junction of Green Lane and Windmill Balk Lane.

A third phase of development, known as Woodlands Central, began in 1920 under the auspices of the Adwick Urban District Council which had been created in 1915. This development extended from the Great North Road in a north-easterly direction along Windmill Balk Lane, Cemetery Road, Woodlands Road and Princess Street to Villa Road. This area was extended north-eastwards in 1927 along four more streets as far as Doncaster Road. Woodlands Central by then consisted of more than 560 houses.

A fourth extension to Woodlands was begun in 1923 by the newly formed, Industrial Housing Association, a partnership between a number of colliery companies. This was Woodlands East, built between the Great North Road and Doncaster Road. This area was laid out in the form of part of the rim of a wheel (Welfare Road) with five spokes, very simply called First, Second, Third , Fourth and Fifth Avenues, leading to Grange Road and Tudor Road, together forming part of an inner rim. At the eastern end were larger houses built for senior colliery officials. Between Woodlands East and Woodlands Central to the north was a large area of green open space on which playing fields were laid out and a miners' welfare institute was built.

A fifth and final major extension to the settlement took place in the 1950s. This was an estate, called Woodlands New estate, built by Doncaster Rural District Council to the north of Woodlands Central, and laid out like a spoked wheel looking like an enlarged version of the layout of Woodlands East.

What is interesting in view of the innovative design and provision of Woodlands Model Village is that Nikolaus Pevsner in his *Buildings of England: Yorkshire The West Riding*, first published in 1959, after mentioning the pithead baths of 1937 and All Saints church ('good for its date') says that the model estate 'deserves mention' but goes on to say that it 'it does not look any different from so many council estates built on the fringes of towns between the two wars'. Its worth has more recently been rewarded: All Saints church (Figure 7.2), two schools, Woodlands Park, the Miners' Institute on Welfare Road and more than 50 dwellings on Central Avenue, Green Lane, Harold Avenue, Quarry Lane, The Crescent and The Park have been awarded Grade II listed status.

Figure 7.2 All Saints church, Woodlands.

So, where in the early days of the growth of Woodlands did the miners and their families come from? Did they drift eastwards across the South Yorkshire coalfield as new opportunities arose, having served their apprenticeships in the older collieries on the exposed coalfield? Or, as further west, had they been sucked in from all parts of the British Isles as news percolated across the country of new employment opportunities springing up at this new large colliery? Or had they been recruited by the newly formed colliery company from their existing workforce at Hickleton and their collieries in Derbyshire and Nottinghamshire? Or had any miners in those places, having heard news of the sinking of Brodsworth Main simply left their place of work and turned up at Brodsworth Main?

Fortunately, the 1911 census took place less than four years after the opening of the colliery and an analysis of the returns allows some of these questions to be answered. Household structure and places of birth of employed men and boys for 38 households living on Central Avenue and 40 households living on Green Lane in Woodlands Model Village in 1911 have been analysed. Altogether the total population was 444 – 212 on Central Avenue and 232 on Green Lane. On Central Avenue the size of households varied from two to 12, with nine of the 38 households also containing boarders. In Green Lane, household size varied from two to 10 and 18 of the 40 households also contained boarders with one household having five boarders besides the tenant and his wife. One hundred and sixty of the 162 employed men and boys worked at the colliery. The two non-miners were a grocers' assistant and a butcher at the Co-op. In only one household was the head of the household a woman. This was on Central Avenue where the head of the household was a Queen's nurse who had been born in Gloucestershire and lived with her mother. Queen's nurses were district nurses trained and supported by a charity that had originated in 1887 with a grant of £70,000 from Queen Victoria. They worked under a medical practitioner to care for the 'sick poor'.

Turning to the places of birth of the 162 employed men and boys, it is not surprising to find there was only one local man living on these two streets in the model village, a colliery banksman born in Brodsworth. Apart from him there were only 19 other men and boys (11.7 per cent) who had been born in South Yorkshire, the next nearest birthplaces to Brodsworth being Hatfield, Kiveton Park and Swinton. At the other end of the spectrum there was one miner who had been born in Newport on the Isle of Wight, another from Stonehaven in Scotland, two from Wales (from Flintshire and Glamorgan) and three from Ireland (including one from County Longford and one from County Galway). The butcher at the Co-op had been born in St Helier, Jersey, in the Channel Islands! There were also 16 migrants from Staffordshire, 14 of them born in Hanley.

But by far the largest stream of migrant miners had been born in the East Midland counties of Derbyshire (51) and Nottinghamshire (38), that is 55 per cent of all the employed men and boys. In a small number of other families, although the husband came from elsewhere, it is clear that he had migrated to the East Midlands before coming to Brodsworth: one man who had been born in Whitwick in Leicestershre had a wife who was born in Hucknall in Nottinghamshire and the miner born in Stonehaven in Scotland had a wife born in Bolsover in Derbyshire. Thirteen of the employed men and boys had been born in Hucknall in Nottinghamshire. What all this suggests is that they had either been recruited by the owners of Brodsworth Main Colliery or had heard of the new colliery opening and had simply moved north to get better jobs (and possibly accommodation in Woodlands). The recruited miners are examples of what are called sponsored migrants (see Chapter 1). There is also evidence of chain migration when word gets back to a previous home area about opportunities in another place and relatives, friends and former neighbours join the pioneer migrants. For example, the mechanical engineer living in accommodation at Woodlands country house, who had been born in Long Eaton, Nottinghamshire, had his nephew, who was an engineer's pattern maker, living with him; a hewer living on Central Avenue who had been born in Woodhouse on the South Yorkshire border with Derbyshire also had his nephew (also from Woodhouse) living with his family; and in another family, where the husband was a blacksmith at the colliery, and who had been born in South Normanton in Derbyshire, they had a boarder who was fitter in the colliery who had been born in Selston, just three miles from South Normanton.

Maltby

Until 1905 Maltby was a small, sleepy estate village just inside the Magnesian Limestone belt on the road between Rotherham and Tickhill, surrounded by rich farmland and ancient woodland. Most of the inhabitants were tenants and/or estate workers on the Sandbeck estate of the Earl of Scarbrough, who resided at Sandbeck Hall, designed by James Paine between 1766 and 1770 in the Palladian style and surrounded by Sandbeck Park, a large landscaped park designed by Capability Brown between 1774 and 1777. In 1905 the park still contained deer. There were also a few middle-class families living in the village, including Dr Wade at Maltby Manor House, the Ellis family at The Grove (who ran a school) and Colonel Mackenzie Smith and his wife Lady Mabel (sister of Earl Fitzwilliam of Wentworth Woodhouse) at Maltby Hall. But apart from these few incomers, the only strangers that the inhabitants of Maltby would have seen before 1905 would have been tourists in wagonnettes visiting the nearby ruins of Roche Abbey. But in 1905 everything was about to change. In that year the Earl of Scarbrough signed a 60-year agreement with the Sheepbridge (Chesterfield) Coal and Iron Company to mine the coal beneath the Sandbeck estate.

First came the railway upon which the colliery depended for the carriage of the coal to its markets. This was the South Yorkshire Joint Railway, which gave access to existing routes to the north, to the south and to the docks of Hull and Grimsby. It entered the Maltby area from the north-east and cut through the woods with a deep cutting across the valley sides of Maltby Dyke on its way southwards to Dinnington Colliery and beyond. In his autobiographical, *Brother to the Ox* (1940), the Maltby writer Fred Kitchen described the upheaval caused by the building of the railway: the inconvenience for farmers, the blasting and rumbling, the disturbance of wildlife, the building of a new temporary town (Tin Town) for the railway builders, the arrival of navvies and drunken brawls on Saturday night. 'Not since the time of the Danes had our village suffered such an invasion' he wrote. But some villagers took advantage of the situation. Instead of having a card at their front door for tourists stating that tea was provided, they replaced it with another one simply saying 'Lodgings'.

The railway was completed in the spring of 1908 and work then began on sinking two shafts at the new colliery. The Barnsley Seam was reached in number 2 shaft in June 1910 at a depth of 820 yards. This shaft was used for lowering and raising the miners and materials. Number 1 shaft reached the Barnsley Seam in late January 1911. This was the shaft used for raising coal. The Barnsley Seam was the only one worked until the late 1960s when the Swallow Wood Seam was also worked. A third shaft, 1,000 yards deep, was sunk in the 1980s to open up the Thorncliffe and Parkgate seams. The colliery closed in 2013.

As work began on sinking the shafts, work started on the construction of housing for the miners and their families, residential expansion that would transform Maltby from a small village of little more than 700 people in 1901 to 7,657 in 1921, to a large community approaching 17,000 at the time of the 2011 census. The sinkers lived in a temporary settlement called Tin Town in the woods in the pit yard, where there was also a tin school. The first permanent houses of the so-called model village, that was designed by Maurice Deacon and built by a local building company, headed by Herbert Mollekin, were completed in 1910. The first part of the new village comprised two concentric circles on land to the east of the old village and about one mile to the south-west of the colliery. The inner circle contained semi-detached villas, with typical half-timbered front gables also seen for example in Pilley (see Chapter 6) and New Edlington (see below) for senior officials (overmen and deputies), a new Anglican church (Figure 7.3), dedicated on Ascension Day, 16 May, 1912), and a parsonage. At its centre was a bandstand. In the outer circle short rows of terraced houses (eight houses in a row) were built for mining families. The first street in the outer circle was called Scarbrough Crescent in honour of the owner of the land, the Earl of Scarbrough. The other street names in the inner and outer circles commemorate the names of the colliery company directors and local landowners under whose land coal would be mined. The two circles were intersected by four radiating avenues, King, Queen, Duke and Earl. The model village was then extended outwards to fill a roughly triangular area bounded by Morrell Road in the west, Muglet Lane in the east and Victoria Road in the south. In this outer area the rows of terraced houses had gardens, a feature missing in the first part of the new village. All the houses had a downstairs bath and tap in a scullery, and a Yorkshire range and copper in the kitchen. By 1912 more than 500 houses had been built in the model village (Figure 7.4). On Muglet Lane a miners' institute was built and across the lane was a sports ground and pavilion and allotments. A new school, Maltby Crags, on Blyth Road on the western edge of the model village, opened in 1912.

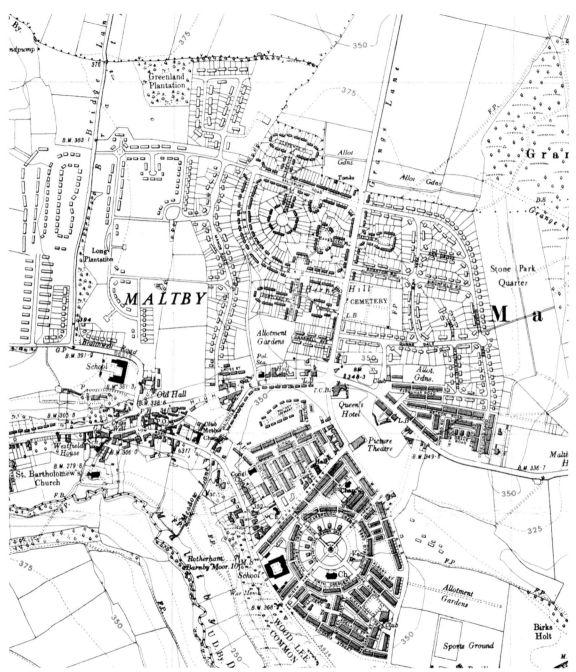

Figure 7.3 The 'Model Village' at Maltby as shown on the Six-inch OS map first published in 1928 with revisions in 1938 and 1948.

Figure 7.4 The Anglican church in the Model Village at Maltby looking towards Firth Crescent. (*Russell Howe*)

The make-up of the population of the model village can be gauged by analysing a sample of the census returns for 1911, the census having taken place on 2 April 2011. Fifty-five consecutive individual household returns have been analysed. These begin in Muglet Lane on the eastern edge of the model village where the enumerator collected the returns from 38 households, before turning onto King Avenue where he collected another seven, then another seven on Scarbrough Crescent and nine on Durham Street.

Muglet Lane was partly made up of households where the employed men and boys worked at the colliery or in the building trade or were shopkeepers or provided other services. The population enumerated on Muglet Lane lived in 38 different households with a total population of 163. Ten of the households contained boarders, with one household containing six boarders. The 38 households contained 64 working men and boys. Forty-three of the working men and boys worked in some capacity at the colliery including six sinkers. Nine were employed in building, presumably the model village, including two builders, five bricklayers and a builder's clerk. One man worked in the brickworks. There were also four shopkeepers (a butcher, a baker, a greengrocer and a newsagent). There was also a policeman and most surprisingly a 'bioscope operator'. A bioscope is an old name for either a cinema or a cinema film, so the bioscope operator obviously showed silent films to the new community before the building of the first cinema in Maltby. Not surprisingly not one of the 64 working men and boys living on Muglet Lane in 1911 had been born in Maltby, indeed only 14 were from South Yorkshire and only four from the rest of Yorkshire. Most of the incomers (28 in all) had been born in the neighbouring counties of Derbyshire, Nottinghamshire, Lincolnshire, Lancashire and Cheshire, but there were also migrants who had been born in London, Surrey, Kent, Devon, Monmouthshire and Nova Scotia in Canada.

The population enumerated in the 23 households on King Avenue, Scarbrough Crescent and Durham Street totalled 118 and contained 42 employed men and boys. Five of the households contained boarders. Thirty-six of the 42 employed men and boys worked at the colliery, including one sinker. The other six were all employed in the building trade – two bricklayers, two carpenters and one builder's labourer. Two of the employed men and boys had been born in Maltby, seven had been born elsewhere in South Yorkshire and another four came from the rest of Yorkshire. Sixteen had been born in Derbyshire or Nottinghamshire and the other 13 had been born in a wide variety of places ranging from Norfolk, to Essex, Berkshire, Oxfordshire and North Wales.

As the colliery went into full production and employed more men, the new village was expanded in 1912 to the north of Tickhill Road on seven straight terraced streets all named after famous admirals of the Royal Navy. On the eastern edge of this development two large villas were built for the manager and under-manager. This was followed in 1914 by the beginning of the building of what became known as 'the poets' estate' (with streets called Burns, Byron, Carlyle, Coleridge, Southey and Tennyson) to the north-west of Morrell Road. In 1922 another estate was built by the Industrial Housing Association to the west of Grange Lane. In 1924, with the creation of Maltby Urban District Council, the building of council housing estates began. After building a few small developments, the large Woodlands estate, containing nearly 400 houses to the east of Grange Lane was begun in 1930 and the Manor Road estate in 1938.

Meanwhile, Maltby's commercial sector expanded rapidly with shops, public houses and clubs springing up, largely along High Street and Morrell Street. There were also two cinemas, the Globe on Carlyle Street and the Picture Palace on Muglet lane. A new park, now called Coronation Park, was also created to the south of Tickhill Road, between Hoyland Street and Muglet Lane and a lido and paddling pool on the Crags Meadows just to the west of the model village. Rapid population growth also demanded more schools and in 1926 Maltby Hall Schools were opened for senior children and then in 1940 a Roman Catholic school was opened. Perhaps the most important educational event was the opening of Maltby Grammar School on the site of Maltby Hall in 1932. This school became Maltby Comprehensive school in 1967 and Maltby Academy in 2010.

House building continued in the post-war period by Maltby Urban District Council, by the NCB, by the Borough Council after its amalgamation into Rotherham Metroploitan Borough in 1974 and by private developers. And as with the street names of the model village, those of some of the newer residential areas are just as remarkable. One area's street names reflect political allegiances (Attlee Close, Cripps Close, Hardie Close, Jowitt Close and Lee Close), while in another the street names are of explorers, Columbus, Magellan and Scott rub shoulders with the astronauts Armstrong and Aldrin.

Because of the colliery's very recent closure (2013), the visitor approaching Maltby from the direction of Tickhill along the Tickhill Road is still presented with a view of a naked colliery spoil heap, now a very rare sight in South Yorkshire.

New Edlington

New Edlington was designed and built to accommodate the families of miners who worked at the nearby Yorkshire Main Colliery (known until *c*.1909 as Edlington Main). The new village was laid out, entirely in brick, along both sides of Edlington Lane beside the colliery (which lay on the eastern side of the lane) between the tiny limestone-built villages of Old Edlington to the south and Warmsworth to the north. The Staveley Coal & Iron Company Ltd, already the owners of Hickleton Main and Brodsworth collieries, had acquired the rights to mine the coal beneath nearly 6,000 acres of land on various contiguous country estates in the Edlington area, the biggest acreage belonging the the Battie-Wrightson family of Cusworth Hall. The colliery site was just to the south of the eastern section of the Dearne Valley Railway that had opened in 1908. Sinking began in December 1909. A detached house and four semi-detached houses were built just outside the pityard to house the families of the senior officials in charge of the sinking. The Barnsley Seam was reached in the summer of 1911 and coal production began in 1913.

Meanwhile work had been progressing on designing and building a new mining village, New Edlington. The first part of the new village was planned to be laid out to the west of Edlington Lane with ten east to west parallel streets running off Edlington Lane to the north of Martin Wells Farm and another four east to west parallel streets to the south of the farm. The Doncaster builder appointed to construct the village encountered financial difficulties shortly after commencing the project and only part the two northernmost east-west streets, Staveley Street and Victoria Street, were begun.

At the time of the 1911 census, which took place on 2 April, the only buildings that had been erected and occupied in New Edlington were the five houses on Edlington Lane for the senior 'sinking' officials and 66 houses on Staveley Street (Figure 7.5). An analysis of the census returns in 1911 for New Edlington is interesting in that it allows a glimpse of the structure of the 'sinking community' before mining proper began. And what must be remembered is that householders themselves for the first time filled in their own census forms.

Collectively, the five houses built for the senior officials were called Yorkshire Main Colliery and contained a population of 28. At the detached house lived William Bunting who described himself as the colliery manager. His 23 years-old son, also lived there. He was a colliery surveyor. In the first semi-detached house lived George White, master sinker, who also had living with his family a boarder who was described as a 'stationary engine man sinking pit'. The second semi-detached house was occupied by a colliery enginewright and his two sons, one a colliery electrician and the other an engine cleaner. The third semi-detached house was the home of

Figure 7.5 Staveley Street, New Edlington.

another enginewright and he and his wife shared the house with two boarders, one a colliery banksman and the other a sinker below ground. The fourth semi-detached was the home of an electrical engineer above ground. Of the eleven working men living in these five houses, two were from South Yorkshire (Swinton and Sheffield), two of the boarders did not know their place of birth and the other seven were either from Derbyshire (five) or Nottinghamshire (two).

Staveley Street's 66 houses contained a population of 373 with household size varying from two to 14. The 14-person household contained the occupant's family together with six boarders, all described as labourers at the colliery, none of whom knew where they had been born. On Staveley Street lived 118 working men and boys of whom 116 worked either at the colliery (101) or constructing sidings and a branch railway (15). The two exceptions were a farm servant and a florist's errand boy. Forty-one of the colliery workers described themselves as pit sinkers, sinkers or excavators. The others described themselves mainly as hewers or colliery labourers.

The places of birth of all these inhabitants of Staveley Street in 1911 are very revealing. Writers in the past have claimed that most pit sinkers were Irish immigrants. Not in this case. Only one pit sinker recorded that he was born in Ireland – in Kilkenny – and he was the only Irishman out of the 118 working men and boys living on the street in 1911. Eight of the workers had been born in South Yorkshire and 15 in the rest of Yorkshire. Most had been born in the East Midland counties of Nottinghamshire (14), Derbyshire (7) and Leicestershire (6), suggesting recruitment by the Staveley Coal & Iron Company. And as usual there were men and boys who had travelled very long distances from their original birthplaces to Staveley Street. There were migrants from Kent, Sussex and Somerset in southern England, from Clapham in London, Edinburgh in Scotland, from Merthyr Tydfil in South Wales and Gwynaesgor in Flintshire in North Wales. The last mentioned, Joseph Pritchard, was clearly one of the migrants who had come to South Yorkshire following the flooding of Mostyn Colliery in 1884 to join his fellow Welshmen working at Old Carlton Colliery near Barnsley (see Chapter 4). He had living with him three children all born in Carlton.

In 1910 a new company, the Edlington Land & Development Company, had taken over the task of building the new village and the layout was redesigned. This time, the main area to the north of Martin Wells Farm would be centred on an east to west tree-lined Main Avenue containing blocks of houses in twos and fours leading to a new Anglican church (St John the Baptist). At the eastern end of Main Avenue on Edlington Lane a parade of shops was to be provided. Running off Main Avenue northwards were three curved crescents and southwards three straight streets, all with blocks of houses in fours, sixes and eights. Each house had a small front garden bounded by a stone wall topped with iron railings and some had overhanging porches to the front door, others had bay windows and most had pointed gables. In 1913 a school was built at the western end of Victoria Road, the *York Hotel* was built on Edlington Lane, opposite the pit gates, and large areas north of the new village were laid out as allotment gardens. During the First World War the new village was extended to the south of Martin Wells Farm, two of the streets being called Thompson Avenue and Dixon Road after Thompson & Dixon, the building company involved. These houses have now been demolished. Bungalow Road to the north of Dixon Road is so named because of the erection here in the early 1920s of War Ministry wooden bungalows that remained there for thirty years.

The appearance of the colliery headgear and chimney stack, the emerging new village and the large influx of migrant miners and their families may have pleased the colliery company directors but it did not please all the local residents. It is said, for example, that the tenant of Warmsworth Hall in 1914 left the village 'on the grounds that the coal mine at Edlington had ruined both the view from the hall and the character of the village (cited in Botterill, 1966, p.34).

By 1921 the population was over 5,000. The housing conditions in the new village at that time were strongly criticised both by the the local sanitary inspector and by Sir Patrick Abercrombie in the Doncaster Regional Planing Scheme report of 1922. Sir Patrick said that the new village 'leaves nearly everything to be desired in its planning and the way the work has been carried out'.

Bearing these criticisms in mind, further housing developments, built to a higher standard than hitherto, continued during the 1920s and 1930s. These included housing built by Doncaster

Figure 7.6 (a) New Edlington in 1930 as shown on the Six-inch OS map and (b) inset: semi-detached house for senior officials.

Rural District Council on Auburn Road and Hazel Road to the north of Bungalow Road; by the Housing & Town Planning Trust on Baines Road and Carr Avenue to the south of Thomson Avenue and by the Industrial Housing Trust between Edlington Lane and Broomhouse Lane to the south of the colliery. In the latter development three of the streets carry the name Markham after Charles Paxton Markham (1856–1923), chairman of the Staveley Coal & Iron Company. By the beginning of the 1930s more than 1,400 houses had been built in New Edlington (Figure 7.6). Another parade of shops and a second hotel, the *Royal Hotel*, were constructed on Central Terrace to serve the southern part of the village, and an open-air market was laid out on Edlington Lane opposite the entrance to Queen's Crescent. And across the road in 1921 the village cinema opened.

This was followed in the mid-1920s by a Methodist church and a Roman Catholic church. Nor had leisure, recreation and sport been forgotten. A large area to the north of the colliery was acquired for the Miners' Welfare Institute, together with a large recreation ground that included a football ground and a cricket ground complete with pavilion. Off Edlington Lane, backed by the colliery headgear, was an open air swimming pool with poolside changing rooms!

By 1951 the population was over 8,500. Housing continued to be built by Doncaster Rural District Council in the 1950s and by the NCB in the 1960s. The mine closed in 1985. A private housing estate was developed on the former colliery site itself in the1990s. Since that time the population has declined slightly and at the time of the 2001 census stood at 8,276. An exciting project on the the edge of the village is the Martinwells Lake Project, where a former clay pit of Edlington brickyard where the bricks that were produced from 1913 to build the new village, has been converted into an amenity area. Fishing has gone on there for many years and the area was declared a Site of Special Scientific Interest in 1989 because of its geological interest. But it remained unmanaged and was the site of illegal tipping. Since 2009 a voluntary friends' group has done a sterling job to protect the site and make it an attractive and easily accessible public amenity area.

New Rossington

New Rossington, about four miles south-east of Doncaster, grew up as the colliery village associated with Rossington Main Colliery. Sinking of this colliery by the Rossington Main Colliery Company, a partnership between the Sheepbridge Coal & Iron Company from North Derbyshire and John Brown & Co, the Sheffield steelmakers, began in 1912. The first coal was raised in 1916. Three coal seams were exploited: the Barnsley Seam, Dunsil Seam and Swallow Wood Seam. In 1927 the colliery changed ownership when it became one of the four constituent collieries of Yorkshire Amalgamated Collieries Ltd. It remained in this ownership until nationalisation in 1947. The colliery was closed by the Coal Board in 1993 but in the following year it was leased by the private mining company RJB Mining who bought it two years later. The colliery eventually closed in 2007.

Prior to the sinking of the colliery the Rossington area was still part of rural South Yorkshire, little changed from almost a century earlier when it had a population of just 383 (in 1821) and was described by Joseph Hunter as 'a pleasant tract of open country' (Hunter, 1829, p. 66). There had been little change during the nineteenth century and by 1901 the population of Rossington had in fact declined to 342. The colliery was sunk about a mile and a half to the west of the tiny village of Rossington, dominated by its parish church, St Michael's, and two miles north-west of Rossington Hall set in its park. The owner of Rossington Hall, Richard James Streatfeild, J.P., (note the odd spelling of his name) lived in rural splendour served by his agent who lived at Mount Pleasant, his bailiff who lived at Home Farm and his gamekeeper whose residence was The Kennels. The only sign of modernisation was the Great Central Railway that ran from south-east to north-west between Rossington village and what would become the site of the new colliery. But all this was to change with the opening of the colliery. On 1 August 1913, the *Doncaster Gazette* announced 'a pastoral calm which had brooded for so long over the woods and meadows around Rossington was already giving place to the hustle and bustle that came in the wake of colliery enterprise.'

The colliery was located just to the west of Holmes Carr Great Wood and the new mining settlement of New Rossington was laid out on the farmland between the eastern edge of the wood and Rossington village. Most of the first part of the new settlement lay in the triangle of land between West End Lane in the north and Grange Lane in the south (Figure 7. 7). At the centre of this new settlement was a mainly residential layout in the form of four concentric circles: the inner circular street which overlooked a 'village green' is called appropriately enough, The Circle. Here were the largest houses, built for senior colliery officials, and St Luke's church. The second circle has a new name for each quarter of its circumference, called Deacon Crescent, Fowler Crescent, Ellis Crescent and Firth Crescent. M. Deacon, Sir Charles Ellis and Bernard Firth were all directors of Rossington Main Colliery Limited and R.W. Fowler was a director of the Sheepbridge company. The third circular roadway runs along the backs of the houses facing onto the second and fourth circular roadways. This also has four names: Edgar Lane, Argyll Lane, Scarbrough Lane and Victoria Lane. The fourth and outer circle also has four separate names. Norman Crescent, Streatfield Crescent, Foljambe Crescent and McConnell Crescent. Sir Henry Norman

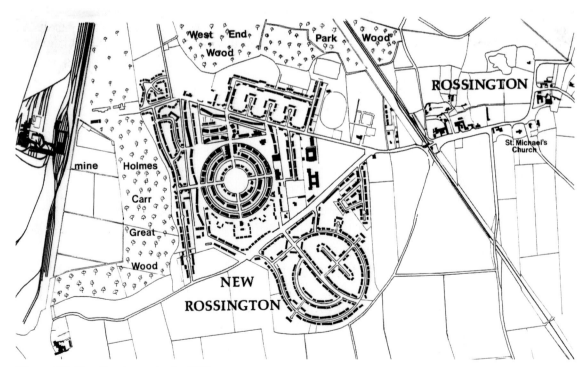

Figure 7.7 New Rossington in the 1930s.

and W.H. McConnell were directors of Rossington Main Colliery Company and Richard James Streatfeild was a local landowner whose home, as noted above, was Rossington Hall. Foljambe Crescent was also named after a local landowner. Cutting through these four circular streets were four radial avenues called King, Queen, Duke and Earl. Bounding the circular development on the west running north to south is King George's Road and on the east, again running north to south was Queen Mary's Road indicating clearly the period when the settlement was built. King George V, who is commemorated in the street name, reigned between 1910 and1936 and his queen was Princess Mary of Teck. More residential streets on the west and north were built surrounding this multi-circular development. To the east, north of West End Lane, stood the Miners' Welfare Hall and behind that stretching northwards to Park Wood were laid out, and they still survive, a play area with a bandstand, bowling green, tennis courts, cricket ground and football ground. To the south of West End Lane, facing the multi-circular development beyond Queen Mary Road and Grantham Road, two schools were built (now Pheasant Bank Academy).

Subsequently a second, bigger, circular estate was built to the south-east of the original development. The design of this development is a little more complicated than the first estate. It has an outer circular road (Aberconway Crescent and Allenby Crescent), a central road cutting through from north-west to south-east (Central Drive), a semi-circular inner crescent (Haig Crescent) and two interlocking streets (Tudor Street and Cross Street). Significantly, the name Aberconway Crescent was named after the 2nd Lord Aberconway, who was chairman of Rossington Main Colliery Company. At the time that the colliery settlement of New Rossington was being created, Lord Aberconway was having a large new family home built in Mayfair in London.

In the first twenty years of mining at Rossington Main, the population grew at a prodigious rate and by 1931 was 9,547 and New Rossington had all the accoutrements of a small town. It had a cinema (the Hippodrome), the *Royal Hotel* (which according to Kelly's Directory of 1936 had an 'excellent cuisine'), a branch of Doncaster Co-operative Society and branches of the National Provincial Bank and the Yorkshire Penny Bank, a motor engineer, who was also a cycle and radio dealer and numerous other privately-owned shops.

Later still, as the colliery employed more and more men, the new settlement expanded southwards and, most extensively, eastwards, at first with council housing and later with private developments, across the railway and eventually as far as the former hamlet of Littleworth with the building of the Littleworth Park estate in the 1970s. In the process, the ancient village of Rossington was completely enveloped with private housing. By 2011 the population of New and old Rossington stood at 13,577. And development continues. Planning permission was given in 2011 to extract coal from the colliery tips, remove the waste and landscape the 120 acre former colliery site. In 2015 the first stage of a large new housing development began. It is anticipated that the site will eventually contain more than a thousand houses, a pub, a hotel, a food store and a primary school.

Epilogue

It has been an interesting journey. From west to east; from the late eighteenth to the twenty-first century; from unplanned to planned; from pre-industrial to post-industrial. But it has not only been an industrial revolution. Over the long period in question there have also been architectural, sanitary, demographic and social revolutions. Not only has the landscape been transformed but so have the lives of millions of people. People today seem to be more aware of the colonisation of the United States, Canada, Australia and New Zealand than of their own local region. Mining migrants came from every county in England, from Wales, Scotland, Ireland and even from overseas to populate the mining villages of South Yorkshire. The descendants of those migrants now consider themselves to be true Yorkshire men and women.

The last colliery, Hatfield Main Colliery, closed at the end of June 2015. But the spoil heap still remains there as it does at Maltby, where the colliery closed in 2013. Elsewhere the 'coil tips' have gone or have been clothed in woodland, as at Dodworth, Skiers Spring and Elsecar and appear now to be part of the natural landscape. Also gone are almost all of the headgear and chimneys. Exceptions include the pumping engine at Elsecar and the headgear at Barnsley Main and Hatfield Main (granted Grade II protected status as recently as November 2015), which stand as memorials to our mining past. Most of the former colliery sites, including the spoil heaps, have been landscaped and either turned into community woodlands or parks, industrial estates, business parks or new housing estates. Many of the public houses, cinemas and even non-conformist chapels that were once thronged with local people have been demolished or converted to other uses including Chinese restaurants, carpet warehouses or gymnasia. And many of the economically active residents in the former mining villages commute to work elsewhere.

So what remains? Well the places themselves in most cases. But some like Concrete, Mitchell Main, Carlton Long Row and the village in the pit yard at Wharncliffe Silkstone Colliery have gone completely. At least in a substantial number of the former mining villages it is still possible to see miners' welfare or colliery officials' clubs and lovingly worked plots in allotments. The most moving features that are dotted throughout the coalfield are the monuments to people, to collieries and to coal mining communities. These include, for example, the monuments to those lost in pit disasters such as the Huskar Pit monument in Silkstone churchyard commemorating the lives of 26 children and young adults killed when the mine was flooded in 1838, the monument in Darfield churchyard to those lost in the explosion at Lundhill Colliery in 1857, the monuments at Ardsley and Kendray commemorating those lost in the Oaks Colliery explosion in 1866 and

Graham Ibbeson's sculpture in Conisbrough that pays tribute to the miners who lost their lives at Denaby Main and Cadeby Main collieries. Much more common are winding wheel monuments announcing that you are entering a former mining village or marking the site of a former colliery. And, of course, there are the brass bands.

The mining way of life has now gone forever. The poem below says it all.

The Final Shift

"Filthy neet" says his unspoken nod
As the homeward miner disappears
Ungreased gates groan on my pit top plod
And the dank sky weeps and hides my tears
And the tormented tree's thirst is slaked
As its branches sweep and the sky is scraped
And the teeming clouds unfold and roll
On this final shift to cut the coal.

Unspoken nods on this filthy night
That rage defiance in dust dark tears
Beneath in the glow of pit shaft light
The spirit that will endure the years
Caged men but proud in shivering gloom
Go tunnelling down to King Coal's tomb
And the clouds above unfold and roll
On this final shift to cut the coal.

And I was one, loving and rearing
Grafting, sweating, playing for the team
Hugged and crying, laughing and leering
Finding the seam and living the dream
The glowering storm foretold the plight
For miners' families from that night
And the troubled clouds unfold and roll
From that final shift to cut the coal.

Steven J. Tye
September 2015

Sources, References and Further Reading

Anon (n.d.) *A Brief History of Concrete Cottages*, People and Mining.

Auckland, C. (1989) *The Growth of a Township: Maltby's Story*, Rotherham MBC, Libraries, Museum & Arts Department.

Botterill, R.E. (1966*) Part of the Lower Don Valley region: A Study of Economic Growth*, special study, Sheffield City College of Education,

Clayton, A. K. (1973) *Hoyland Nether*, Hoyland Nether Urban District Council.

Clayton, A. K. (1995) The Newcomen-type Engine at Elsecar', in B. Elliot (ed), *Aspects of Barnsley: Discovering Local History*, Volume 3, Wharncliffe Publishing Ltd, pp. 133–48.

Coates, B.E. and Lewis, G.M. (1966) *The Doncaster Area*, British Landscapes Through Maps series, Geographical Association.

Cooper, S., Chesman, R. and Jones, M. (1990) *Church, Chapel and Community: Thorpe Hesley and Scholes in 1840*, Holy Trinity Church, Thorpe Hesley.

Dataller, R. (1925) *From a Pitman's Notebook*, The Dial Press.

Dataller, R. (1934) *Oxford into Coal-Field*, J. M. Dent & Sons Ltd.

Dearnley, J. (n.d.) *The History of the Ancient Parish of Darton*, unpublished manuscript in Barnsley Archives and Local Studies Library.

Dinnington and District History Society (2007) *Dinnington Days Gone By*, Arc Publishing and Print.

Dodsworth, A. (1995) 'The Odd Confounded Speech of Rawmarsh Lane': Aspects of the Growth of Parkgate 1831–1891', in M. Jones (ed), *Aspects of Rotherham: Discovering Local History*, Wharncliffe Publishing Ltd, pp. 175–205.

Dodsworth, A (2014) *Gwennie's Diary: A Kiwi's World Tour to Yorkshire 1939–40*, Fonthill Media Ltd.

Elliott, B. (2001) *Britain in Old Photographs: Royston, Carlton & Monk Bretton*, Sutton Publishing Ltd.

Elliott, B. (2001) *Britain in Old Photographs: Darfield & Wombwell*, Sutton Publishing Ltd.

Elliott, B. (2001) *Images and Scenes of Old Worsbrough*, ACCS Enterprises.

Fleming, A. (1995) 'Coal in the Valley: Coal Mining in the Dearne Valley at Wath', in M. Jones (ed), *Aspects of Rotherham: Discovering Local History*, Wharncliffe Publishing Ltd, pp. 220–40.

Fleming, A. (2012) *Wath Upon Dearne – Artistic Views: Landscape & History*, Wath Community History Group.

Fordham, D. (2009) *Brodsworth Colliery, Woodlands & Highfields: Early Development*, Fedge-el-Adoum Publishing.

Fordham, D. (2009) *Askern Main & Instoneville: Early Development*, Fedge-el-Adoum Publishing.

Fordham, D. (2009) *Bullcroft Colliery, Carcroft & Skellow: Early Development*, Fedge-el-Adoum Publishing.

Fordham, D. (2014) *Bentley Colliery & Bentley New Village: Early Development*, Fedge-el-Adoum Publishing.

Fordham, D. (2014) *Yorkshire Main Colliery & New Edlington: Early Development*, Fedge-el-Adoum Publishing.

Fordham, D. (2015) *Maltby Main Colliery: The Development of a Mining Community*, Fedge-el-Adoum Publishing.

Fordham, D. (2016) *Denaby & Cadeby Main Collieries: The Development of a Mining Community*, Fedge-el-Adoum Publishing.

Glister, R. (1996) 'The Conception and Construction of the Barnsley Canal', in B. Elliott (ed), *Aspects of Barnsley: Discovering Local History*, Volume 4, pp. 215–24.

Goodchild, J. (1986) *Coals From Barnsley*, Wakefield Historical Publications.

Goodchild, J. (2001) *Images of England: South Yorkshire Collieries*, Tempus Publishing Ltd.

Handley, C., Stapleton, B. and Rowles, A (2007) *Shire Brook: the Forgotten Valley*, ALD Design & Print, on behalf of Shire Brook Valley Heritage Group.

Hearne, R (1995) 'Roger Dataller of Rawmarsh' in M. Jones (ed) *Aspects of Rotherham: Discovering Local History*, Wharncliffe Publishing Ltd, pp. 298–308.

Hey, D. (1981) ' Industrialized Villages', in G.E. Mingay (ed) *The Victorian Countryside*, Routledge & Kegan Paul Ltd, pp. 353–63.

Hill, A. (2001) *The South Yorkshire Coalfield: A History and Development*, Tempus Publishing Ltd.

Huddlestone, J. (1995) *A Geography of Childhood*, Chapeltown & High Green Archive.

Hunter, J. (1828–31) *South Yorkshire*, J. B. Nichols & Son.

Jackson, S. (ed) (1988) *Industrial Colonies and Communities*, The Conference of Regional and Local Historians in Tertiary Education.

Jones, J. (ed) (1980) *Glimpses of High Green's Past*, Ecclesfield Adult Education Centre.

Jones, M. (1966) *Changes in Industry, Population and Settlement on the Exposed Coalfield of South Yorkshire 1840–1908*, thesis submitted to the University of Nottingham for the degree of Master of Arts, October 1966.

Jones, M. (1980) 'The Mapping of Unconsidered Trifles: A Yorkshire Example', *The Local Historian*, Volume 14, Number 3, pp. 156–63.

Jones, M (1993) 'The Thorncliffe Riots 1869–70', in B. Elliott (ed), *Aspects of Barnsley: Discovering Local History*, Wharncliffe Publishing Ltd, pp. 179–92.

Jones, M. (1994) 'A Welsh Diaspora and a South Yorkshire Colony: the establishment of a Welsh Community in Carlton and Smithies', in B. Elliott (ed), *Aspects of Barnsley: Discovering Local History*, Volume 2, Wharncliffe Publishing Ltd, pp. 49–72.

Jones, M. (1996) 'Combining estate records with census enumerators' books to study nineteenth century communities: the case of the Tankersley ironstone miners, c.1850', in D. Mills and K. Schürer (eds), *Local Communities in the Victorian Census Enumerators' Books*, Leopard's Head Press Ltd, pp. 200–16.

Jones, M. (1998) 'St Thomas's Day & Collop Monday', *Yorkshire Journal*, 24, Winter 1998, pp. 66–9.

Jones, M. (1999) 'Denaby Main: the Development of a South Yorkshire Mining Village', in B. Elliott (ed), *Aspects of Doncaster*, Volume 2, Wharncliffe Publishing, pp. 122–42.

Jones, M. (2000) *The Making of the South Yorkshire Landscape*, Wharncliffe Books.

Jones, M. (2003) 'Model Communities or Squalid Living? Exploring the History of Mining Villages', in M. Jones *South Yorkshire Yesterday: Glimpses of the Past*, Smith Settle, pp. 143–52.

Jones, P. (1969) *Colliery Settlement in the South Wales Coalfield 1850 to 1926*, University of Hull, Occasional Papers in Geography, No. 14.

Joy, D. (1975) *A Regional History of the Railways of Great Britain, Volume 8, South and West Yorkshire*, David & Charles.

Kitchen, F. (1940) *Brother to the Ox*, J. M. Dent & Sons Ltd.

Lodge, T. (1996) ' A Midland Railway Branch in South Yorkshire' in B. Elliott (ed), *Aspects of Barnsley: Discovering Local History*, Volume 4, pp. 225–53.

Lodge, T. (1998) 'Coal for Commerce: Sustaining a Manufacturing Economy', in M. Jones (ed), *Aspects of Rotherham: Discovering Local History*, Volume 3, pp. 170–88.

MacFarlane, J. (1972) 'Essay in Oral History – Denaby Main – a South Yorkshire Mining Village', *Bulletin of the Society of Labour History*, pp. 82–100 (volume 25) and 39–42 (volume 26).

MacFarlane, J. (1978) 'Counter- Offensive for a South Yorkshire Mining Community', in R. Harrison (ed), *Independent Collier: The Coal Miner as Archetypal Proletarian Reconsidered*, The Harvester Press.

Marshall, J. D. (1993) 'Industrial Colonies and the Local Historian', *The Local Historian*, 23:3, pp. 146–54.

Medlicott, I. R. (1999) ' John Curr, 1756–1823, Mining Engineer and Viewer', in M. Jones (ed), *Aspects of Sheffield: Discovering Local History*, Volume 2, Wharncliffe Publishing Ltd, pp. 63–78.

Orwell, G. (1937) *The Road to Wigan Pier*, Victor Gollancz.

Parish, A. (n.d.) A History of Pilley, *unpublished typescript*.

Taylor, H. (1994) 'Nails, Mules, Music and Miners: Village Life in Mapplewell and Staincross through the Nineteenth Century', in B. Elliott (ed), *Aspects of Barnsley: Discovering Local History*, Volume 2, Wharncliffe Publishing Ltd, pp. 97–126.

Taylor, P. (1992) 'There were fields all around us: Thurcroft in the 1920s', Part 1, in *Ivanhoe Review*, No. 2, Spring 1992, pp. 11–19.

Thomas, J. (1844) *Walks in the Neighbourhood of Sheffield*, Robert Leader.

Index